The Believer's Spiritual Development Manual

Growing the Believer into Spiritual Maturity

By Stanley Ivey

Published by: Learner Series LLC.

LEARNER
Learners inherit the earth

Learner Series
P. O. Box 7073
Grand Rapids, MI 49510
Tel: (616) 805-6146
Email us at getpublished@att.net
www.learnerseries.com

Unless otherwise indicated, Bible quotations are taken from the King James Version.

Published in the United States of America

Table of Contents

Dedication v

Foreword vii

Acknowledgements x

Introduction.. 1

PART 1: Born Again: What's that? 5

PART 2: Understanding the Growth Process........................... 11

PART 3: The Goal of Spiritual Growth.................................. 21

PART 4: Functions of the Spirit, Soul and Body 25

PART 5: Deeper Lessons on the Mind 36

PART 6: The Laws of the Human Spirit 48

PART 7: How to Train the Human Spirit 56

PART 8: How to Dress the Human Spirit............................... 62

PART 9: Gifts of the Holy Spirit I Corinthians 12:1–11.............. 75

PART 10: The Gifts Versus the Fruit of the Spirit...................... 81

PART 11: Understanding Spiritual Authority 88

PART 12: The Word Made Flesh Today 100

PART 13: The King and Kingdom Principles 103

PART 14: The Law of Honor 108

PART 15: Managing Friendship and Relationships 112

Concluding Thoughts 114

Glossary 115

Reference List 121

Dedication

This book is dedicated to my lovely wife **Stacy**, son **Joshua** and daughter **Joanna** for their continued patience as I spent time studying, reading and writing over these years. May the Lord continue to bless and prosper each of you.

Watchman Nee – I am heavily indebted to him for his insight and book "Spiritual Man." I am encouraged to have something for believers to read for years to come as I am reading his material years after his passing – I am truly blessed by his insights. I read his books like a mentee listening to a mentor who left me a living legacy.

God is the Author of growth and development in every area of life. Christian growth and maturity, however, is not automatic or instant; but intentional and takes time.

But grow in grace, and *in* the knowledge of our Lord and Saviour Jesus Christ. To him *be* glory both now and forever. Amen (2 Pe 3:18).

Eph 4:11-14 And he gave some, apostles; and some, prophets; and some, evangelists; and some, pastors and teachers; (12) For the perfecting of the saints, for the work of the ministry, for the edifying of the body of Christ: (13) Till we all come in the unity of the faith, and of the knowledge of the Son of God, unto a perfect man, unto the measure of the stature of the fullness of Christ: (14) That we *henceforth* be no more children, tossed to and fro, and carried about with every wind of doctrine, by the sleight of men, *and* cunning craftiness, whereby they lie in wait to deceive;

Foreword

The Word of God declares in John 16:13, "Howbeit when He, the Spirit of truth, is come, He will guide you into all truth." In "The Believer's Spiritual Development Manual", Overseer Stanley Ivey has opened up Kingdom truths not commonly written to the church nor spoken in the church. In his writing, Overseer Ivey is both transitional and transformational. As we are encouraged to transition our thinking to that of an intense examination of our minds, we truly are beyond the mediocracy that has caused the carnality that is too common in our churches especially among leadership. As our thinking changes, there is a transforming of our external actions to come into obedience with the will of God. Overseer Ivey progresses from the thoughts of the mind to the relationship of our human spirit with the Spirit of God. This level of accountability requires us to not just look holy, but to be holy. This book should be read by all, for as we progress in the last days, we need revelation knowledge to achieve being doers of the Word of God, and not hearers only. I pray God takes Overseer Stanley Ivey all over this globe to not just share the word which came from his heart to the pages of this book, but to speak to the nations which is in need of a voice of integrity with a life that precedes.

Apostle Jeffrey Kearney
Church of the New Covenant
343 Dodd Street
East Orange, New Jersey 07017

Reverend Stanley Ivey has devoted himself to the ministry of the Christian gospel, as a pastor, in hard grounds in Jamaica, W.I. He is a man of humble spirit, calm demeanour, and devoted to learning. He attracts thinkers in both the young and the mature and when one leaves his presence they are usually challenged to live a life that has a deeper relationship to God. I am also delighted to have a personal acquaintance with him.

I am reminded that Jude 1:3 states that Christians are to "earnestly contend for the faith". This highly suggests that every believer has a responsibility to fight for their beliefs which was entrusted to all believers. In addition, we are to be ready to give an answer to every man that questions the hope that is within us (1 Pe 3:15). However, to do so, every believer must know why they believe, what they believe, and how to intelligently communicate that belief. There is a dearth of knowledgeable Christians.

Our response, to date, has been one of nationalism, ethnocentrism, and whatever the latest self-help book, philosophical podcast, or popular thinking offers. The Word of God is held as irrelevant, and out of touch with reality and does not form the crèche of moral ethics for our society. Skilled attackers, adept scientists, and lettered theologians continue to erode the precepts held valuable by our forefathers simply because we are not proficient and diligent in our learning of the Word of God.

It is this arena that the Believer's Spiritual Manual engages. The potential ministry of the Church is unlimited when Christians are tutored in the "hope of their calling" (Eph 1:18). Furthermore, a revolutionary idea will take root when believers no longer see their assembly as a weekly event, but will view themselves as the body of Christ. The result will include those who are without a call becoming aware of their calling; those who did not know their gifts will awaken to their gifts; and those who did not identify as part of the community will be integrated into the body as full citizens of the Kingdom of God.

It is my view that the Believer's Spiritual Manual, written by Reverend Stanley Ivey, serves to enrich the life of the believer and expand the ministry of the Church. This will be the work that you will reach for consistently refreshing and renewing your mind towards the Word of God. The Believer's Spiritual Manual – a great reference bolstering the believer to "earnestly contend for the faith."

Cheryl A McGibbon, Evangelist
Naba Hokmah Ministries
Teaneck, NJ 07666
Written on the campus of Princeton Theological Seminary, 13 November 2016

Acknowledgements

I want to acknowledge my **Lord and Saviour Jesus Christ** for his continued grace and goodness in my life. I thank him for choosing me to be a shepherd and equipper of the saints. Thanks to **Sophia Gabriel – Bailey** who heard me minister on some of the things in this book at her church. She came after the services and was the first person to encourage me to put the teachings into book form, noting I could not preach and teach all the things in depth as I would love to do due to time constraints.

Romel Gordon who encouraged me to start writing my teachings and insights so that others can benefit from what God invested in me.

Dr. Donald A. Roberts who published his quality books in a short span of time. It encouraged me to finish up this book that I had started years earlier.

Rev. Philbert Johnson, who taught me the foundations of the Faith. For his confidence and sacrifice in my personal growth and development as a servant of God.

Apostle Jeffrey Kearney and Evangelist Cheryl McGibbon for writing a foreword and offering valued suggestions in the process.

Dr. Bill Winston – a mighty man of faith and vision.

Rev. Phillip (John) Smith – who said we should record and package what God gave us for his people so others can benefit in years to come, even long after we are gone – sound words.

Evangelist Claudette Williams – who helped to discuss and probe spiritual matters as I served as her Pastor.

Windsor Heights New Testament Church of God Members who supported and loved my ministry. You really believe in my gift to preach and teach God's Words.

Blackwoods and Thompson Town New Testament Churches of God members - you showed keen interest and gave meaningful interactions as I taught portions from this book in Bible studies.

Leighton Taylor - each time he heard me preach he would come asking, "When are you going to write the book?" Thank you for the encouragement.

Richard Wright – he gave me some insightful ideas to pursue as a pastor and how to put this book and other projects together.

Pauline Raymond – a woman of prayer and deep spiritual understanding. She gave me Spiritual Man by Watchman Nee which changed my life permanently.

The late **Dr Myles Monroe** who taught us to die empty - don't die with an unpublished book, article, poem and so forth. You remain a blessing to the Kingdom of God.

To the many unnamed persons who encouraged and supported me in the publishing of this book.

Introduction

I am delighted to introduce to you this very special manual that is intended to equip each believer for a deeper walk with God. It will be beneficial to every believer no matter their level of maturity in the Faith. Initially, my focus was on new believers, but I realize in expanding the topics covered it will serve *both immature and mature alike.* The chapters are arranged to show the developmental stages that believers go through until we become mature in the Faith. As you read through this manual, you will discover material that speak directly to the inner man or how the born again spirit is matured. It deals with key areas that cannot be dismissed or ignored if one desires to grow and be all that God intended you to be. You will notice that some regular emphasized topics are not covered in this manual, like the importance of attending church regularly and how to approach Bible Studies. This was intentional because I do feel that the majority of believers know there importance and they are usually taught to new believers on a whole. My intention is to build on such a foundation and go deeper into spiritual growth and development.

Believers, in these last days, need deeper levels of clarity and discernment in spiritual matters or else we are left exposed to satanic deception. Some things cannot be detected by higher education or by having theological training – only by learning spiritual laws will we be delivered. Pray and depend on the Holy Spirit to teach you deeper and further than I went. Do not become too critical of believers you know or yourself for that matter, who have not yet attained your level. Just make it your aim to learn, keep growing and teach as many as you can – God will give you the opportunity once you are prepared.

The term manual is chosen because one should read and practice and reread this material until it becomes a part of one's lifestyle. We all face on a daily basis, one way or another, spiritual warfare or temptation to give in or compromise our walk of faith. If you are a new believer, seek your pastor or bible teacher who should know how to explain further any concept or term I use in this manual. It was for this fact, I initially wrote for teachers and leaders who need solid literature or study material that can be used in training believers from conversion to a fruitful walk of faith.

If you doubt any of the revelations or illuminations I shared, just ask God to open it to you. This is critical. I heard things as a new believer, and dismissed them as foolishness or heresy. But, lo and behold, the Holy Spirit taught me the same things, which I dismissed. I would not believe had he not shown or spoken to me personally. As a born and bred Pentecostal believer within the New Testament Church of God in Jamaica, I had questions about people who were deemed filled with the Spirit who were hard to get along with and some who would get into quarrels and kept malice after speaking in tongues and bringing a word of knowledge in the service. I was very puzzled and concerned because I wanted the infilling they had. But I could not understand how a person who was filled with the Holy Spirit could live like that. Others were deemed mature once they got filled or spoke in tongues – some of whom came to Christ years after I did. Thank God for my Pastor and spiritual father, **Rev. Philbert Johnson**, who taught me the foundations of the Faith – without love for God and each other we are only going through the motions or spiritual gymnastics. As you read this manual, **do personal retreats, take rest, do reflections, repent where necessary, realign or reposition yourself, return to God's work, reengage in your assignment**

and release others into their calling and purpose in God. Above all, feed and develop your true self – your **Born Again Spirit or the Inner Man**. That is what will outlive the body into eternity. Enjoy the journey and be empowered to know Christ and make him known.

PART 1: Born Again: What's that?

To begin our discussion, let us go back to the beginning when man was created. We read in Genesis 2:7 "And the LORD God formed man of the dust of the ground, and breathed into his nostrils the breath of life; and man became a living soul." When the spirit made contact with the body, the soul was produced. The soul is the link between the body and the spirit (two realms – natural and supernatural); hence man is a tripartite being consisting of: spirit, soul and body. By the spirit we make contact with the spiritual world and with the Spirit of God, both receiving and expressing the power and life of the spirit realm. Hence,

1. The **spirit** makes us **God-conscious.**
2. The **Soul** makes us **Self-conscious** (Mind, Will and Emotion).
3. The **Body** makes us **environmentally** conscious.

After the creation of man God proceeded to lay down his law for Adam to follow. In Genesis 2:9 onwards we read:

> And out of the ground made the LORD God
> to grow every tree that is pleasant to the

sight, and good for food; the **tree of life also in the midst of the garden**, and **the tree of knowledge of good and evil**....16 And the LORD God commanded the man, saying, Of every tree of the garden thou mayest freely eat: 17   But of the **tree of the knowledge of good and evil**, thou shalt not eat of it: for in the day that thou eatest thereof thou shalt **surely die**. (KJV emphasis added)

The Fall of Man

God gave Adam a free will or the capacity to choose and make decisions.   Watchman Nee said, "Man in his original state was neither sinful nor holy and righteous. He stood between the two **(e.g. Neutral – he could reverse-disobey God and die or Drive - obey God and live forever).** "He went further by saying, "If he would exercise his will by taking and eating of the fruit of life, **God's own life undoubtedly would enter his spirit, permeate his soul, transform his entire inner man, and translate his body into incorruptibility. Intellect** was [one of] the chief cause of the fall; hence in order to be saved one must believe in the folly of the Word of the cross rather than depend upon his intellect (1Co 1:18-31; 1 Pe 2:24)." **(Emphasis   added)** (1968, pp 44-47) Disobedience severed the link with God in the spirit - ADAM CHOSE DEATH. "Death of the spirit is the cessation of its communication with God. Death of the body is cutting off of communication between spirit and body."

(Nee, 1968, p. 50)

Born Again: In Short - GOD

After repentance of a believing sinner God:

1. Forgives and cleanses him from all sins through the blood of Jesus Christ (1 Jhn 1:7-10).
2. Sanctifies and justifies him – makes him innocent before Him (God) in Christ Jesus (Rom 5:1; 1Co 6:11).
3. **Reconnects** the believing sinner's **spirit** with **his SPIRIT** (I Co 6:17).
4. Indwell him with His Holy Spirit – **imparting new life** to his spirit (Jhn 14:17; Rom 8:14-17).
5. The Holy Spirit baptizes him into the Body of Christ (called Baptism of the Holy Spirit) (1Co 12:13).
6. God is working to renew his mind through the WORD (Rom 12:1-2).
7. Will transform his body at the return of Christ/the resurrection (Php 3:20-21).

Please note that Adam before and after the fall was not "born again." No one, for that matter, in the Old Testament was "born again." Not even our Lord Jesus Christ was "born again." He was the last Adam, from Heaven. His **Human Spirit** was not in a fallen state, so he could hear and be led by the Holy Spirit as Adam did before the fall. There is a lot of ignorance in this area of theology; but I insert it here for good measure.

WE ARE NOT:

Sinners saved by grace. We were sinners and we were saved by grace as a fact of our past. Our present and future is different now that we are new creation in Christ. Let us not confuse the fact that Christians sin with them being sinners instead of saints of God. Sinning is a sinner's lifestyle because of the fallen nature in him; while holy living is the lifestyle of believers. A believer's sin is an error or failing in his/her walk. It cannot be a lifestyle for anyone who is a believer.

Sinners who fall down and got up. Our born again experience or new birth changed who we were in essence; not just our getting up after we fall. We got up or risen with Christ to walk in the newness of life. The person who fell and the one who got up are two different persons before God.

Worm, dust and ashes before God. Terms like these express man who is outside a relationship with God and Christ Jesus our Lord. God only referred to Adam as dust after he sinned or after the fall of man.

Only a lump of clay… to name a few. None of which is Biblical. They only speak to what **we were**; not who **we are**. A believer is now the image of God restored in Christ. Man was taken from the dust which gave him his body; but he had a spirit connected to God. I know persons say some of the above things to express humility; but to contradict what God said about you as a believer is ignorance, not humility.

Don't just go by what people tell you; study the Bible/Word for yourself. Here are a few things the Word of God said we are:

1. Born again or From Above (Jhn 3:1-9).
2. Sons of God (Rom 8:14-17).
3. Heirs of God and Joint-Heirs with Christ (Rom 8:14-17).
4. Raised up with Christ (Eph 2:6).
5. Seated in Heavenly Places in Christ (Eph 2:6).
6. Redeemed and made alive in the last Adam (Rom 5:12-21; I Cor 15:20-22, 45).

7. Have a new nature – the seed (sperm) of God in us (1Jhn 3:9).

8. We have peace in Him (Rom 5:1).

9. We are righteous in Christ (2 Co 5:21).

10. Blessed with all spiritual blessing in Christ (Eph 1:3; 2 Pe 1:3).

11. Citizens of Heaven and the Kingdom of God on earth (Php 3:20-21, Col 1:13).

12. A part of the Body of Christ (1Co 12:13).

13. Partakers of His divine nature. I can now walk in the spirit (2 Pe 1:3-4).

14. A part of the Bride of Christ (Eph 5:30-33).

PART 2: Understanding the Growth Process

KEY – KNOW WHO YOU ARE IN CHRIST; DIFFERENT FROM WHO YOU WERE AS A SINNER

The Lord enlightened my understanding of spiritual growth and its processes by using a very well known verse from Proverbs 22:6 "Train up a child in the way he should go: and when he is old, he will not depart from it." He said I should "TREAT THE SPIRIT MAN AS YOU WOULD A NATURAL BABY. SEE THE BORN AGAIN SPIRIT AS A NEW BORN BABY THAT NEEDS TO BE FED, TRAINED AND DEVELOPED INTO AN ADULT. IT DOES NOT MATTER THE AGE, NATURALLY, OF THE NEW BELIEVER, HE OR SHE IS A NEW BORN." If a new believer is developed properly in the faith, he or she will have an authentic and meaningful walk with God. This will be the effective and proper way to deal with backsliding trends of new believers from churches. Don't blame it all on the parable of the sower and the seed. We will study the spiritual growth process under three headings: Little children, Young men and Fathers. These were drawn from First John 2:12-14,

> I write unto you, little children, because your sins are forgiven you for his name's sake. 13 I write unto you, fathers, because ye have known him that is from the beginning. I write unto you, young men, because ye have overcome the wicked one. I write unto you, little children, because ye have known the Father. 14 I have written unto you, fathers, because ye have known him that is from the beginning. I have written unto you, young men, because ye are strong, and the word of God abideth in you, and ye have overcome the wicked one. (emphasis added)

Little Children

There are other terms used in the Bible for young or immature believers. I will highlight some of these term under this heading. To be born again, as taught in John 3:3- 8, means to be born *"from above."* The Greek word for again is *"anothen"* found fourteen times in the New Testament and the KJV translated it five different ways, namely: above, again, top, beginning, first (**see glossary**). It was never used to denote repetition of action, deed or event or simple to say one more time. This birth has never taken place until that moment in time. It is a new birth; but radically different from the natural birth. **Regeneration** (*palingenesia*) only found in Matthew 19:28 and Titus 3:5 and literally means a "new birth." It is a compound word, "*palin-genesia.*" "*Palin*" means "*again,*" as in one more time, regarding something that was done previously. "*Genesia*" from the word "*genesis,*" which speaks of birth or nativity. Paul used the term "babes in Christ" designating one who needs milk (1Co 2:3; Heb 5:12-14). In Second Corinthians 5:17 he said, "Therefore if any man *be* in Christ, *he is* a **new creature**: old things are passed away; behold all things are become new." Apostle John mentioned that the little children sins are forgiven for his name's sake and they have known the father (1Jn 2:12-13).

At this level of growth:

1. The new believer is newly born of the Word of God or Seed of God. First Peter 1:23 "Being born again, not of corruptible seed, but of incorruptible, by the word of God, which liveth and abideth for ever."

2. The new believer needs the milk – predigested spiritual food. As newborn babes, desire the sincere milk of the word, that ye may grow thereby: (1Pe 2:2).

3. The new believer needs "spiritual parents" in the Lord to nourish, care and nurture him in the Lord.

4. The new believer is aware spiritually; but lacks spiritual understanding or comprehension.

5. The new believer can't properly feed him or herself with the word (rightly dividing the word).

6. The new believer can't properly cleanse him or herself with the word (read and apply properly).

7. The new believer can't walk properly or consistently – he or she will do things not knowing they are wrong. **Patience and care must** be demonstrated in order not to get discouraged.

8. The new believer can't talk properly – they will be ignorant of the Word and many Christian terminologies. They will need the foundation lessons mentioned in Hebrews 6:1-2, "Therefore leaving the principles of the doctrine of Christ, let us go on unto perfection; not laying again the foundation of repentance from dead works, and of faith toward God, of the doctrine of baptisms, and of laying on of

hands, and of resurrection of the dead, and of eternal judgment."

9. The new believer will need to be taught the importance of **attending various services or the assembling of ourselves together.** Hebrews 10:25 "Not forsaking the assembling of ourselves together, as the manner of some *is;* but exhorting *one another:* and so much the more, as ye see the day approaching."

10. The new believer will need to be taught the importance of **fasting, prayer, Bible study and meditation as a matter of principle.**

11. The new believer will need to be taught the importance of **The Renewing of the Mind** (Rom 12:1-2).

12. The new believer will need to be taught the importance of giving to the Lord financially and other wise. This includes *tithes and offerings, giving and receiving, sowing and reaping in the Kingdom of God.*

Young Men

At this level issues of Identity will come to the forefront. I am no more a child or babe in Christ; but **WHO AM I REALLY?** You grasp some history of yourself as a Christian; but **WHERE EXACTLY AM I**

GOING? WHAT IS IT THAT GOD WANTS ME TO DO? There are seven areas that are critical to spiritual maturity. These stages were patterned after *Flow Chart of The Spiritual Maturation Process.* The headings and contents are not the same; just the progression.

1. **Bible Knowledge** – knowledge of the Bible is sought not just publicly; but privately as well. A desire for deeper knowledge is on the increase.

2. **Bible Understanding** – the Bible is coming together and has more perspective. Rightly dividing the word of truth is developing well and confidence on the increase. The Bible is studied more consistently in private.

3. **Thought Life** – The Word of God is now challenging your thinking process. The renewal of the mind begins to cause conflicts internally with what was usually ok; but now it's not.

4. **Walking with God** – a better understanding is gained of **creeds versus deeds, confession versus conduct, and belief versus behavior**. Motives of persons are now becoming clearer.

5. **Love Walk** – The two greatest commandments are now coming into focus: love for God and

neighbor. Do we love God for who he is or are we just trying to escape hell fire. Our love for the brethren and unbelievers are becoming more important.

6. **Handling Trials and Testing** – you now realized that God is involved in all your trials and testing moments in order to develop your character. Satan does not have freedom to do with us as he likes.

7. **Dealing with Weaknesses** – weaknesses are not just about breaking sinful habits; but insecurities concerning God and the Bible. An attack on the Bible from false teachers can call his or her faith and commitment into question. Hence some persons backslide or join groups with cultic doctrines and tendencies all because they were not properly planted or grounded in the Word.

John said young men have overcome the wicked one, they are strong and the word of God **abideth** in them.

Fathers

Fathers are more advanced in the seven areas that are critical to spiritual maturity

1. **Bible Knowledge** – Bible study is a part of daily lifestyle. You are able to think and analyze the Word with a very good grasp. Bible content is now very familiar so you can think through several passages without reading them immediately to grasp more dimensions of truth.

2. **Bible Understanding** – God pours out rivers of spiritual understanding. In Eph 1:18 Paul prayed that "The eyes of your understanding being enlightened; that ye may know what is the hope of his calling, and what the riches of the glory of his inheritance in the saints," There's nothing you can't quickly, fluently grasp. Your spiritual senses are fully exercised and you are feeding on the meat of the word (Heb 5:14). The Bible RULES your life.

3. **Thought Life** – God's thoughts are now your thoughts through the Word. The battlefield is now under your control – the mind is the battlefield according to Second Corinthians 10:3-5. You now make Philippians 4:8 your moment by moment thoughts, "Finally, brethren, whatsoever things are true, whatsoever things *are* honest, whatsoever things *are* just, whatsoever things *are* pure, whatsoever things *are* lovely, whatsoever

things *are* of good report; if *there be* any virtue, and if *there be* any praise, think on these things."

4. **Walking with God** – your life is now synchronized: **creeds and deeds, confession and conduct, belief and behavior have now come together**. Issues of motives for doing things are now God centered.

5. **Love Walk** – There is a deep love for God and his will for your life. Paul said, "For to me to live *is* Christ, and to die *is* gain" (Php 1:21). You now fully understand why the fruit of the Spirit – love, is more important than spiritual gifts (I Co 13:1-3).

6. **Handling Trials and Testing** – trials and testing are viewed as God continuing to perfect us in him. Obedience is learnt though suffering (Heb 5:8). The character of God in you is more important than personal comfort.

7. **Dealing with Weaknesses** – being knowledgeable is good and it reveals personal weaknesses. **Your battles are not just about choosing right over wrong; but between good and better.** It is not just doing the right things; but doing things right. How do you give up things you have done for many years in order to handle deeper issues while dealing with those who think you are losing it? You want to be in the centre of God's will. You

want to leave an indelible mark or legacy for the next generation while you raise up youth in the faith to take over.

PART 3: The Goal of Spiritual Growth

What is it that God wants to see when he looks into the earth realm? The plan of God, from the beginning, is to have a multiplication of himself in the earth realm. Man in God's image, after his likeness is what God intended to do before the entire **Angelic Realm**. Angels were not created in God's image and angels don't multiply in numbers – they don't procreate as humans do. God had a different plan or assignment in the creation of man. God was *"duplicating"* himself when he made man. Man was created after the God kind; while everything else was created after their kind or its kind.

Adam's descendants were to be born in righteousness and without a fallen, sinful nature. In this way, God would have seen a whole nation of Sons of God. In Christ, we were born again or from above, not of corruptible seed. Seed is from the Greek word "sperma" depicting the fact that we now have God's DNA newly implanted in us. Peter said, in First Peter 1:23 "Being born again, not of corruptible seed (*spora*), but of incorruptible, by the **Word of God**, which liveth and abideth for ever." *"Spora"* speaks of that which is scattered as descendant, hence the term

Diaspora. The "Word" is God, "In the beginning was the Word, and the Word was with God, and the Word was God" (Jhn 1:1). John also said, "Whosoever is **born of God** doth not commit sin; for his seed (*sperma*) remaineth in him: and he cannot sin, because he is born of God" (1Jn 3:9). **This seed grow into God's fullness in us.** Ephesians 4:15 said "But speaking the truth in love, may grow up into him in all things, which is the head, *even* Christ." This growth is to have Christ formed, like a baby in the womb, in us. Galatians 4:19 "My little children, of whom I travail in birth again until Christ **be formed** in you." We should grow stronger over time, in Him. Ephesians 4:14 "That we *henceforth* be no more children, tossed to and fro, and carried about with every wind of doctrine, by the sleight of men, *and* cunning craftiness, whereby they lie in wait to deceive." Spiritual growth is expressed in our stability.

Our **speaking should change**, **First Corinthians 13:11** reads, "When I was a child, I spake as a child, I understood as a child, I thought as a child: but when I became a man, I put away childish things." **Our understanding** should be as man or mature, First Corinthians 14:20 Brethren, be not children in understanding: howbeit in malice be ye children, but in understanding be men. Speaking of Jesus, Paul said in **Colossians 1:15**, "Who is the image of the invisible God, the firstborn of every creature." Hebrews said, "Who being the brightness of *his* glory, and the express image (*eikōn*) of his person... (Heb1:3)" The term *"eikōn"* means, "the *figure* stamped, that is, an exact *copy* or [figuratively] *representation*): - express image. (Strong's Concordance). **When God completes us, he will see millions of Sons.** There is one "only begotten" Son, which came from the Greek *"monogenes"* which really meant "UNIQUE" or "ONE OF A KIND" in the Gospels. Later in the epistles, believers are called sons of God. Romans 8:14 said, "For as many as are led by the Spirit of God, they are the sons of God." Jesus is now referred to as firstborn among many brethren. "For whom he did foreknow, he also did predestinate *to be* conformed to the image of his Son, that he might be the firstborn among many brethren." Romans 8:29 Jesus is first of many, yet supreme to all. **God wants millions of Sons** to have full dominion now and in the age to come. **Sons of God CANNOT LIVE A SINFUL LIFE**, "Whosoever is born of God **doth not commit sin**; for his seed (*sperma*) remaineth in him: and **he cannot sin**, because he is born of God"

(1Jhn 3:9) (emphasis added).

Sons of God walk in the spirit daily and therefore, they don't fulfill the lust of the flesh. According to Galatians 5:16, it is impossible to fulfill the lust of the flesh while walking in the spirit. "This I say then, Walk in the Spirit, and ye shall not fulfill the lust of the flesh." **Shall not** is stated with a double negative in the Greek text (*ου μη*) depicting an impossible scenario.

We now understand that at conversion we receive a new nature like that of Jesus Christ. We are to grow in grace and knowledge of our Lord and Saviour Jesus Christ unto a perfect man, unto the measure of the stature of the fullness of Christ. This maturity is a full reflection of Jesus Christ in us. As a consequence, we live our lives free from sin and its dominion. We will now study in more details how the born again spirit in the believers function and how to grow in a spiritually mature person.

PART 4: Functions of the Spirit, Soul and Body

Here are some passages to study as a believer until God give you enlightenment: Genesis 2:7; First Corinthians 14:14-15; First Thessalonians 5:23; John 4:23-24. There are many others scriptures; but these are used as the guiding passages. Many times we focus on knowing about God, Satan, Demons and not who we are as human beings and more as, **Born Again Believers**. If you know who you are, everything about you will change: You will understand five things better:

1. **Yourself better** – how to live in the victory Christ won for us on the Cross.
2. **Your Bible better** – God's blue print for life.
3. **The Spirit Realm** – Where God and His angels, Satan and demons live alongside us in the natural visible world of the senses.
4. **Spiritual warfare better** – how we enforce the victory that is already won by Christ for us and it is ours in Him. **We fight from victory; not for victory**.
5. **That God's order is Spirit, Soul then body**. Our spirits are already brand new and full of the life of

God. God works from inside out; while we work from outside in – here lies a huge difference in spiritual life and understanding.

"Spiritual warfare is the counsel of the human mind by any other spirit, other than the Spirit of God because your frequency level is low" (Dr. Cindy Trimm). Believers need to be very careful and certain that the counsel they are following is that of the Spirit of God or that the voice we claim we hear is really that of God. We must know that God, Satan and demons speak to the believer through thoughts. Thoughts must be examined against the Word of God and be in line with the Word of God, before they are accepted as from God. The Apostle Paul said we are to be, "Casting down imaginations, and every high thing that exalteth itself against the knowledge of God, and bringing into captivity every thought to the obedience of Christ; (2Co 10:5). This can only be done through prayer, studying of the Word and leaving in obedience to the written Word of God – the Bible. We will now learn how the human spirit is to cooperate with the Spirit of God in our daily lives.

The human spirit has three broad functions noted by Watchman Nee: They are: Intuition, Communion and Conscience. Each function will be explained below.

The Spirit (human) functions or purposes.

Please bear in mind we have corresponding spiritual sense just as we do in the natural, for example, the spirit can hear, see and so forth on a spiritual level. The more we understand and develop these functions, the more equipped we are as believers to discern and execute God's perfect will.

Intuition – spiritual sensing is called intuition. It is our ability to *hear the voice of God or to hear from God*. It is *our spirit hearing from God's Spirit*. Spirit understands spirit. Our *born again spirit* has no desire to sin or displease God. Therefore, it is those who walk in the born again spirit that overcome sin and the devil. These believers are referred to as spiritual, rather than carnal. Here are some points to ponder about intuition:

1. It comes without **Reason or Cause. It is not human activated.**
2. Comes **direct to your spirit** from the Holy Spirit.
3. Enables us to "hear" God and Know his Will.
4. The voice of the Spirit is usually very soft; it cannot be heard unless it us listened to attentively with everything else quieted.
5. It frees you or Restrains you – without you understanding why.

6. An unuttered and "soundless" voice telling us YES or NO. Corresponding to the High Priest's Breastplate. No – Urim (light), Yes – Thummim (perfection) in the Old Testament.

7. It passes all understanding (Php 4:7). It is an inward knowing that you can't fully explain because your mind can't fully grasp what is happening until a revelation is given to the mind from the Spirit of God.

8. It gives us Discernment in spiritual matters. We discern spirits, God's truth from error or false doctrines. See (mind and spirit relationship for more details).

Communion – This is the ability to worship God. Intuition enables us to hear from God while communion enables us to respond to God appropriately in worship and adoration. Our born again spirit can now relate freely to God on a daily basis. Here are some ways communion functions in our lives as believers:

1. God is Spirit - true worshippers worship God in spirit and in truth (Jhn 4:23-24). Our born again spirit is now able to have a relationship with God.

2. The (Holy) Spirit bears witness with our (born again human) spirit that we are sons of God (Rom

28

8:16). We are one (neuter one) spirit with Christ (1 Co 6:17). What Christ did we now can do through him in us – **I am still grasping this revelation as I write. John 14:12,** "Verily, verily, I say unto you, He that believeth on me, the works that I do shall he do also; and greater *works* than these shall he do; because I go unto my Father."

3. I will pray with the spirit (1 Co 14:14-16). This is a higher way to pray. Having your spirit speaking directly to God in a language supplied by the Holy Spirit. There are multiple benefits of this for each believer, such as, it builds up the believer in faith (Jud 1:20). It edifies or builds up the believer individually and allows the believer to speak mysteries with his/her spirit (I Co 14:2, 4). It is an eye opening and life changing revelation the Lord gave me years ago, that can benefit both Pentecostal and Charismatic believers.

4. I will sing with the spirit (1 Co 14:14-16).

5. I will bless with the spirit (1 Co 14: 14-16).

6. The spirit gives us utterance (Act 2:4). Utterance means the ability to speak at two levels:

      a. **Natural** – to deliver a word or message or to preach the gospel with boldness

b. **Spirit given** – speaking in tongues as in the Book of Acts and First Corinthians 12 -14.

We have learned that intuition and communion give us a good communication and relationship with God. We will now look how conscience fits into our walk with God.

Conscience – controls and tells us right and wrong without a written text. Conscience gives us a sense of good judgment. God's laws written within us in the beginning, but got marred after the fall of man and started to be restored at conversion. Here are some more things to ponder or comprehend about the conscience:

1. It is our first reference to determine right from wrong.
2. The spirit correcting and reprimanding us, rendering us uneasy when we fall short of the Glory of God.
3. Reproves sin and approves righteousness. When He (Holy Spirit) comes he reproves… (Jhn 16:8).
4. It must be cleansed by the Blood of Jesus from dead works (Heb 10:22).

5. If it condemns you – repent where necessary (Rom 8:1, 33-37).

6. **To be faithful to conscience is the first step of Sanctification.**

7. **To be faithful to conscience gives us access to the spirit realm.**

8. Conscience doesn't argue with us.

With the knowledge of the functions of the spirit, we will now look at those of the soul.

The Soul – The soul is usually referred to as our Mind, Will and Emotions. Let's look at each element of the soul to bring more clarity and how it defers from the spirit.

Mind (the battlefield) – with the mind we reason, think, analyze and rationalize things. "A confused mind cannot walk in the spirit, there has to be clarity to walk in spiritual authority" (T.D. Jakes). The mind has three broad functions:

I. **Memory** - the ability to retain or revive in the mind past thoughts, learning, beliefs, images, ideas, etc. The mind functions as a store house and memory brings out what was stored previously – good or bad. *Memory replays the past.*

II.   **Imagination** - the power to form (conceive or picture) mental images of what is not actually present. *Imagination pre-plays the future.*

III. **Reasoning** - The ability to draw conclusions or inference from assumed facts.

Will – Makes decisions, ability to choose based on what your mind or spirit reveals.

Emotions – express our feelings, affections, passions, love, anger, hurt, sadness – not physical.

We will now see how the Holy Spirit works in and with us to secure our victory. He does not work in spite of us. We must be led by him; not forced. **The Holy Spirit – He will lead us into all truth.** He needs **four** main things to operate effectively in us:

1. **A Born Again Human Spirit** – a place of residence, a place to live and operate from.

2. **The Written Word – Spiritual Manual.** He does **nothing that will violate the Word. The Word and the Spirit are one. Anyone who is walking in full obedience to the Word is walking in the Spirit. Anyone who is walking in the Spirit will walk in obedience to the Word – there is no exception to this RULE.**

3. **A Renewed Mind** – that knows intimately the Word. It will understand revelation and illumination from God. An un-renewed mind in a believer is problematic in the Kingdom God. It is a basis of enmity with God. **A new spirit needs a new mind that will correspond with faith and understanding. Jesus said, "New wine needs new wineskins" (Mat 9:17). The more the mind is renewed, the more revelation and or illumination flood it.**

4. **Faith in our hearts (Heb 11:1, 6)**

We now understand how the human spirit and soul must be properly aligned with the Holy Spirit. This will then lead us to bring our bodies under full subjection. The body should only express the wishes of God through the spirit and soul.

PLEASE KEEP IN MIND THAT EACH SENSE - FUNCTION HAS A SPIRITUAL CONTERPART TO IT.

I.   **The Body (senses)** – types and shadows of spiritual reality

1. **Eyes** – see first tangible things. I was praying one night and I started seeing lovely things so I opened my eyes only to realize the place was still dark – I was

33

upset with myself and this happened more than once. My spiritual eyes were looking.

2. **Ear** – picks up audible things in the natural and spiritual realms.

3. **Nose** – Picks up what cannot be seen or heard. Gift of Discernment, God breathe into the nostrils; not the mouth (Gen 2:7).

4. **Mouth** (5 main functions) –

   i. **Taste** (and see) when you taste your eyes see (Psa 34:8).

   ii. **Teeth To eat** – to chew on the meat of the word.

   iii. **Speak** – death and life are in the power of the tongue (Pro 18:21).

   iv. **Show affection** – kiss.

   v. To **Form things** – God created and rules His world with His Words (Heb 11:3).

5. **Skin – establish contact, temperature.** Establish a safe environment. One can sense the presence of demons or opposing forces in a service at times.

We have seen how spirit, soul and body accomplish the will of God in us. The Holy Spirit helps us to learn and walk in obedience to God on a daily basis. We now know how to hear and respond to God according to his word and express the same through our bodies. Hence we should present our bodies as living sacrifices unto God, holy and acceptable to Him (Rom 12:1).

PART 5: Deeper Lessons on the Mind

Previously, we looked at Memory, Imagination, and reason for the mind. Now we will take a deeper look on the mind. We will learn how the mind must work with the Holy Spirit's wisdom and revelation in our walk with God.

Laws of the Mind (Rom 8:5-6; I CO 2:9-16)

1. The Holy Spirit reveals God's Will to the Human Spirit.
2. The Human Spirit reveals it to the mind, which comprehends the meaning of this revelation.
3. The will engages his spiritual strengths to activate the body that it may execute God's will.
4. Nothing in a person's life is closer to the spirit than his mind.
5. The mind learns the spiritual and material realms.
6. Whatever the mind is set on, the man walks after.
7. Mind perceives mental knowledge.
8. God leads us; not force us.

9. If we want to live a full life our minds must be renewed. Too many cannot undertake anything with their heads.

Minds that give Satan and Evil Spirits Room to Work

1. **An Unrenewed Mind** – The Devil's best workshop. They had it before salvation and still have occupancy or control. Sinful patterns and thinking remains and exalt itself against the Knowledge of God.

2. **An Improper Mind** – If a child of God cherishes sin in his heart he is lending his mind to satanic spirits for their use. He is helpless to resist evil powers behind whatever sin he allows to persist in his mind. If our mind is full of prejudice towards the truth or the preacher, truth will not enter it nor will it extend to our lives.

3. **Misunderstanding God's Truth** – every time we accept a lie from the evil spirit they are fresh ground to the enemy for further activities against the believer.

4. **Accepting suggestions from the enemy** – about your circumstances and future. Prophesying what we will become based on

our past and or present circumstances. TAKE EVERY THOUGHT CAPTIVE (2 Co 10:2-5).

5. **A Blank mind** – God desires us to understand His Word with the intellect, from whence the emotions, will and spirit are reached. A blank mind cannot think.

6. **A Passive Mind** – The empty head means not using it, whereas a passive one means awaiting some external force to activate it. The mind suffers the onslaughts of the powers of darkness more than any other organ of the whole man. *The peril for the Christian is to have false teaching injected into his thought life so as to lead him astray.* (Nee, 1968, pp 18-22)

Key – We cannot separate temptation and thoughts.

Renewing the Mind (Rom 12:1-2)

Your MIND is renewed when you apply principles. EVERY life battle is a mind battle. Every TEMPTATION MUST pass through the mind. If you win in your mind, you will win in life. If you lose in your mind, you will lose in life. Your self portrait determines your self-conduct; your self-conduct determines your prosperity on earth.

Your mind needs **three things** each day:

1. Your heart and your mind need **Instruction** (WORD of God).
2. Mind needs **FOCUS.**
3. Mind needs a **HERO** – you need a champion that excites you. Your hero decides your energy, endurance and experience (Rabbi Ralf Messer).

Mind and Spirit Relationship

The mind and the spirit must be separated by the WORD until the mind is renewed to work with your new spirit (Heb 4:12). A renewed mind comes back into oneness with the spirit because both contain the newness and the Word of God.

1. The spirit perceives spiritual realities.
2. The spirit gives knowledge and revelation; but these must be kept and used by the mind.
3. The spirit supersedes the mind at all times. Hence the mind can reject what the spirit conveys because it is not renewed to learn and understand.
4. The spirit knows.
5. The mind understands.
6. The mind and the spirit must be satisfied in order to go to the next level.

a. Whenever you hear a doctrine or teaching that is **true**, you need two things to go to the next level:

1. Your Spirit being at peace.
2. **Your Mind understands** – if not let the peace of God which passes all understanding keep/ guard (Php 4:7). My thoughts are higher than your thoughts (Isa 55: 9). You can only use a teaching you understand. In all your getting, get understanding (Pro 4:7).

b. Whenever you hear a doctrine or teaching that is **false or erroneous,** **two of three** things usually happen:

i.   Your Spirit remains or becomes uneasy, troubled or without peace.

ii.   Your Mind understands the teaching. OR

iii.   Your Mind doesn't understand the teaching.

Never leave the final judgment to the mind. The inner, spiritual voice is higher knowledge. Go with your spirit until the mind gets more information or revelation. When you get the revelation or the wrong expose, you will often say, "I knew it."

For example, in recent years a certain Bible teacher predicted the year, month and Day of Judgment. I felt very uneasy in my spirit about the prediction; but I decided to have an open mind as a Bible teacher and examine the teachings. I then went on YouTube and listen to the entire series on the end times, which was over ten hours of teachings. Our congregations looked at the prediction and we did a series on the end times. Personally I understood the calculations and how he explained the scriptures; but my spirit could not accept the teaching. The year, month and day came and no judgment day. He said it would be six months later and that too was past. All I could say at the end of all the distress it caused those who believed the error was that *"I knew it"* was wrong from the first time I heard it. My spirit raised an alarm from the day I heard the teaching – you should have the same experience.

7. We must have an open mind to preachers and teachers of the WORD. Truth must first pass through the intellect before it reaches the spirit. Your spirit can hear, accept a word from God, rejoice about it; but your mind still may not figure it out until long after. Sometimes only after more direct prayers and more studies the veil is removed. Believe me, I sensed and rejoiced

41

over things I could not explain until long afterwards.

Mind and Spirit Prayer

1. Pray with your mind; instead of waiting for the spirit to move.
2. Pray until the spirit rises up slowly within you and take over.
3. Whatever is obtained in the spirit must be preserved and employed by the mind.
4. Pray with your mind until your spirit anoints and response toward what you pray… then flow with the spirit.
5. The mind receives light from the spirit.
6. Demons impose their authority and transmit poisonous thoughts in the mind at times – Guard it diligently, daily, and carefully.

You must learn to pray and seek God, even when you don't sense the anointing on you during prayer. The strengths and determination of the mind is going through further training. In other words, can you still do what God told you to do even when you don't feel like it or don't feel like he is backing you up? It's only a test. I heard somebody said, "**During a test, the teacher is usually silent.**" During an exam, the teacher stops talking or teaching while you do the exam – you are now required to produce or show what you learned.

Principle of Prayer (Gen 1:26; 2:7; Mat 16:19; Luk 18:1)

From the following passages a number of principles can be drawn after careful study. These are only a few of many passages that teach matters relating to prayer and spiritual warfare. They are not the only ones that were used in this section to outline these principles of prayer.

> And God said; Let us make man in our image, after our likeness: and let them have dominion over the fish of the sea, and over the fowl of the air, and over the cattle, and over all the earth, and over every creeping thing that creepeth upon the earth. (Gen 1:26)

> And the LORD God formed man of the dust of the ground, and breathed into his nostrils the breath of life; and man became a living soul. (Gen 2:7)

> Forever, O LORD, thy word is settled in heaven. (Psa 119:89)

> The heavens, even the heavens, are the LORD'S: but the earth hath he given to the children of men. (Psa115:16)

> And I will give unto thee the keys of the kingdom of heaven: and whatsoever thou shalt bind on earth shall be bound in heaven: and whatsoever thou shalt loose on earth shall be loosed in heaven. (Mat 16:19)

> And he spake a parable unto them to this end, that men ought always to pray, and not to faint; (Luk 18:1)

From Genesis we noted that man alone was given dominion on earth. God did not include himself OR angels in the dominion mandate on earth. God said, **"Let THEM** have dominion...." As a result of what God did, man became the legal steward of earth's domain. Man is a spirit, has a soul, and lives in a physical body. Only spirits with physical bodies can function legally on earth. That is the reason Satan "borrowed" the serpent's body to talk to Eve in chapter three. Any spirit without a body is illegal on earth, for example, Satan and demons. Good Angels don't preach the Gospel as men do (Act 10:1-8). They know the message; but were not authorized to preach it as men do. Any influence or supernatural interference on earth is only legal by mankind permission through prayer. This applies also to the evils and demonic operations in the earth realm. Evil men are involved in the releasing of these spirits on earth through our sins and disobedience to God's word. This is happening whether we know it or not, believe it or not.

Prayer is granting God "licence" to operate in the earth. This is so because man was established as a king over the earth. To give dominion to someone, is to confer kingly authority and rule on the individual over a particular territory. In this context, man was given earth. Man was to pray or communicate with God in how he is to govern on God's behalf. In prayer, man exercises his God given authority to invoke heaven's ability on his behalf. When we pray we ought to come in agreement with the Word of God. As a result by the mouth of two or three witnesses every word is established (2 Co 13:1).

Prayer is kingdom activity. In prayer we Bind and Loose as Jesus told Peter in Matthew 16. To bind is to forbid something, declare it unlawful, improper, unfit, to disallow something; while to loose is the opposite. To loose is to declare something fit and proper to be done, to be lawful and permissible. Here is the rule of binding and loosing you should *never forget. It is God who set the rules or settle his word in heaven for ever*. In life and in prayer, we are ONLY permitted to bind what God binds and loose what God looses. *Do not permit or loose something that God bind or forbid. We are permitted to enforce the laws of God; not to set them.* Most translations mistranslated what Jesus said in Matthew 16 and as a result, we assume authority that God did not give. This is *very serious,* because persons speak and feel like God is now our errand man. He does our bidding and not the other way around.

God's Word is Spiritual Law. (Capps 1995, p. 2) The spirit world is controlled by the Word of God (Spiritual Law). The natural world is to be controlled by man speaking God's Word. (Capps 1995, p. 3) Prayer is your legal right to use faith-filled words to bring God on the scene in your behalf, or for another person. (Capps 1995, p.6) *Faith will make prayer work. Prayer won't work without faith; faith will work without prayer.* (Capps 1995, p. 7) Forgive if you have ought against any. Mark 11:25 said, "And when ye stand praying, forgive, if ye have ought against any: that your Father also which is in heaven may forgive you your trespasses." As we pray, we are to depend on the Holy Spirit (Luk 11:13) and learn to pray in tongues – your spirit prays and the Holy Spirit prays through you (Rom 8:26-27; I Co 14:14-15).

Faith is paramount in prayer. Faith is release by words from your mouth (Dr Frederick K.C. Pryce Sr.).

Faith cometh by hearing and hearing by the word of God (2 Co 5:7; Rom 10:17). Faith also comes by or when we hear from God (Dr. David Oyedepo). The Word is what works; not just prayer – faith-filled words (Capps 1995, p. 30). Prayer is acknowledging that we have a partnership with God. Without God man cannot; without man God will not. This is a reason men ought always to pray and not faint. Even when we don't see changes in the natural as we pray, God moves in response to our prayers and if we don't faint, we will have a manifestation. I do hope that you are not only encouraged to pray; but that you will actually pray and start exercising your God-given dominion over evil spirits or demons.

PART 6: The Laws of the Human Spirit

The universe was created and functions by specific laws whether we like it or not, know them or not. If we know them and apply them correctly, they will benefit us at all times. There are laws of the body as it relate to reproduction, eating, work and rest to name a few. The spirit of man is no different. There are eight such laws that I learnt from Watchman Nee which the Holy Spirit re-enforce and taught me further in some areas (Nee 1968, pp. 144-62). We will now look on each of the laws of the spirit as follows:

Conditions of the spirit – state of being/position the spirit is in at any given moment. There are four broad categories a believer spirit may be in at a given point in his/her life and walk with the Lord.

1. **Spirit can be oppressed** or in a decline/backslidden state or below normalcy or cast down. This believer in under demonic assaults or attacks due to a lack of maintenance or spiritual disciplines of prayer and the Word.

2. **Spirit under compulsion** – can't stop freely. Unruly spirit – take everything for joke. The fruit of temperance is absent. **The Believer lost control of his/her spirit** – spirit out of

control (Pro 25:28). A believer should have rule over his/her spirit at all times. Paul said "The spirits of the prophets are subject to the prophets" (I Co 14: 32). The human spirit is in focus here in Corinthians, the Holy Spirit is subjected to no prophet or believer.

3. **The spirit is defiled** – Paul said, "Having therefore these promises, dearly beloved, let us cleanse ourselves from all filthiness of the flesh and spirit, perfecting holiness in the fear of God (2 Co 7:1). Satan gained ground through hardness of heart, pride, envy, jealously, malice to name a few.

4. *Our Spirits should be Quiet and Firm, Free and Light, Flexible and Pliable, Guarded and Ready - being fully clothed with the entire Armor of God (Eph 6:10-18).* The human spirit must be ready to cooperate with and be led by the Holy Spirit. For as many as are led by the Spirit of God, they are the sons of God. (Rom 8:14)

Weights on the spirit – The spirit should be light and floating. Free from Satan's Strongman call the **Spirit of Heaviness** (Isa 61:10). Causes and some effects:

1. Because of our disobedience to God, we create an open door or breach in the armor.
2. It is to stop God's Worship and Work in the church or on the earth.
3. Take away joy and lightness from the believer.
4. Stop the work of the Holy Spirit through our spirit.
5. Spirit gets dull and dim. The believers loose spiritual energy or might.
6. We are to lay aside every weight according to Hebrews 12:1-2.

Burden of the spirit – This is from God for a purpose or an assignment.

1. Comes with a meaning or purpose to work, pray, preach, teach and so forth.
2. Can still worship, pray, preach, sing, teach etc.
3. Joyous to the spirit; but trouble to the flesh. Becomes bitter if resisted or not fulfilled.
4. A sign that God is ready to work in any area manifested: singing, preaching, praying, healing and so forth. It is a sign of UNCTION TO FUNCTION. Remain calm, prayerful and very focus during this time, especially at your place of assignment. The adversary will try to

do or say something to you or through others to throw you off course.

5. Keep your spirit free at all times to hear and receive from God.

Poisoning of the spirit – This person got hit by the fiery darts of enemy. No Breastplate in place (Eph 6:10-18). Persons become poisoned because of hurts and disappointments experienced. It leads to being unforgiving, having hatred and later bitterness which poisons the believer. It will lead to issues, such as:

1. Sorrowful or broken spirit.
2. We become unyielding, narrow and selfish – self interest start to take over due to hurts received.
3. Lead to an unforgiving spirit (Heb 12:15; Son 2:15).
    - Foxes that spoil the vine.
    - Hurts lead to hate and then bitterness.
    - Many backslide – feeling they have good reasons to leave God presence.
    - Fault-Finding and enmity – not from God or the Believer.

4. Pride: can't mix anymore. Pride goeth before destruction, and a haughty spirit before a fall (Pro 16:18).
5. The person can become withdrawn.
6. Everything becomes wrong or a problem.

7. It will lead a person to give up his or her responsibilities in the house of God.

Blockage of the spirit – the spirit needs the soul and body to operate (Mat 11:28). There has to be a flow from God through the believer. A blockage exists whenever this is not the case.

    a. The Soul and Body are outlets for the spirit and the Holy Spirit.

    b. Soul needs to be at rest, but instead:

- The Mind – confused.
- The Will – weary, impotent, can't choose wisely.
- Emotionally disturbed or troubled, easily upset, harsh and bashful.
- Refuse to do things during public services.
- Just want to be alone.
- Feel to give up trying.
- Body – Weak and lazy.

To be free, SPEAK AND BELIEVE THE WORD. Pray it through aloud. There is something about praying for breakthrough boldly.

Ebbing of the spirit – This is a gradual decline in strength and power.

1. Life, strength and power are still present; but not flowing.
   - It takes time to happen.
   - Caused by a lack of maintenance: prayer, the word and fasting.
2. May lose your joy, peace and power. Do not enjoy prayer and the Word of God as before.
3. If one sins – repent immediately and reclaim your flow. We have drawn back – let God reveal it in prayer.

Sinking of the spirit – Caused by Self Centeredness.

Focus on our past experiences, for example, good feelings during a service – need them to return. Want the same methods and things to be repeated. God wants the believers to advance in the spirit realm. But we often love sensual experiences with God, so the enemy provides counterfeit. It is not every supernatural occurrence is of God. Elijah's experience is a case in point,

> "And he (the LORD) said, Go forth, and stand upon the mount before the LORD. And, behold, the LORD passed by, and a great and strong wind rent the mountains, and brake in pieces the rocks before the LORD; but the LORD was not in the wind: and after the wind an earthquake; but the

LORD was not in the earthquake: And after the earthquake a fire; but the LORD was not in the fire: and after the fire a still small voice" (1Ki 19:11-12).

There was a mighty – wind, earthquake and fire; but God was not in them. Moses was told to strike the rock and later to speak to the rock – he struck the rock twice after he was told to speak to the rock. As a consequence he missed the Promised Land (Exo 17:6). Other results may be:

1. Self Centered prayer and worship. What I can get rather than what I can do to bless others becomes the focus.
2. Too much focus on within and not above (Col. 3:1-4).
3. Live after feeling rather than the spirit. No power only "enjoyment."

Irresponsibility of the spirit – the believer's spirit is out of Control. "He that hath no rule over his own spirit is like a city that is broken down, and without walls" (Pro 25:28). A part of the fruit of the spirit is self control. Self control is a key element in all spiritual matters. Other factors to consider are as follows:

1. Spirit not shining. Light of the Lord is the human spirit (Pro 20:27).
2. Disturbed by external forces – can't cooperate with the Holy Spirit.
3. It's not because we are tired, but not spiritually trained.
4. Environment, family, relatives, friends, work all under attack – pray and believe God.
5. The spirit is subject to the prophets (1 Co 14: 32; Pro 20:27).
6. Harden, harsh and unyielding – can't choose properly or follow the Holy Spirit.

Now that you have the knowledge and understanding of the laws of the human spirit, it is now time to train your spirit. Training is needed because spiritual growth and development is not automatic; there is a definite process that one has to go through.

PART 7: How to Train the Human Spirit

The word **Train** means: to develop, strengthen, make strong, firm, sharp and accurate the human spirit. Victory as a Christian does not come automatically. Hence the **Human Spirit or Our Spirit** has to come in proper alignment with the Holy Spirit to live victoriously. The main objectives, of this chapter, are:

- To know how to walk in the spirit and power.
- To know the leading of the Holy Spirit.
- To know the instructions of the Holy Spirit.
- To know God's Perfect WILL for us (Rom 12:1-2).
- To know our will and the Word (God's will).

The headings numbered 1-3 and 5 and some of the sub points were drawn from Kenneth E. Hagin book, entitled, *"How You Can be Led by the Spirit of God"*. All the way through you will notice the centrality of the Word of God in all of what we do.

1. **Meditate on the Word**

   What you meditate on you feed, what you feed, feeds you. Stronghold is a mind resistant to change. "Knowledge of the Word properly applied wins battles." (Dr Frederick K.C. Pryce Sr.)

a. Sinner versus Saint – The word is clear that believers are saints; not sinners saved by grace.

b. The Word gives us a Deeper understanding of ourselves and God.

c. The Word is food and nourishment for the spirit.

d. The Word Transforms the mind – our minds need **REPROGRAMMING or Spiritual Updating**. Three needs of the mind:

    i.   **Needs the word of God** – only the Word must set our limits. If God said it's yours, you can have it. The Word of God cannot and will not fail.

    ii.   **Needs Focus** – focus on the Word. That which you focus on increases in your life.

    iii.   **Needs a Hero** – from the Word, someone who excites you. Someone you greatly admire. Someone that overcame in your area of ministry or battle from whom you can learn or gain mentorship principles.

e. The **Word of God** counteracts Satan's lies, schemes or wiles. The Word of God is TRUTH.

f. My people are destroyed because of lack of knowledge (Hos 4:6).

2. **Practice the Word** – Jas 1:22-26

   Dr Cindy Trimm said, "Do something for thirty days is discipline. Do something for sixty days it becomes a habit. Do something for ninety days it becomes a lifestyle." She further states that, "to reverse one lie – you need to hear the truth at least thirteen (13) times."

   a. Don't be deceived concerning Theology and Doctrine.

      i.   Theology – our views, beliefs or positions educationally about God.

      ii. Doctrine – what we do or practice, how we actually live our lives. We live what we truly believe.

   b. **Be a doer; not only a hearer** (Greek auditor of a course) of the Word. Doing the Word is what brings success and increase. Your faith must not be mental only, it must be lived out daily

      • Jhn 1:14 – Word made flesh, Christ fully formed in us (Gal 4:19).

      • A doer releases the power of the Word.

   c. **The Word works; but you have to work it** (Bishop T. D. Jakes). Act upon the Word and God will honor your obedience. Faith needs works because faith without works (corresponding actions) is dead. Faith needs works to be complete or alive.

d. **Cleanse us** (Psa. 119:11-12); Lamp and light (Psa 119:105).

e. **God watches over his word to perform it** (Jer 1:12). Heaven and Earth shall pass away; but not the Word (Mat 24:35; Mar 13:31).

f. **The Word won't return void** (Isa 55:11).

g. **The Word separate** the Wheat from the Tares

   i. Wheat and Tares look alike during growth.

   ii. When mature the Tare still stands straight up (Pride), Wheat bows down under (Humility) the weight.

   iii. When crushed: Wheat is white on the inside; the Tare is black on the inside.

3. **Give the Word first Place in your Life**

   Solomon said the Word is Life and health (medicine) to all their flesh (Pro 4:20-22). Your allegiance to the Word is a sign of growth and spiritual maturity.

   a. When problems arise, mature believers ask key questions, for example:

      • What does the word of God say about this? or

      • What does the Bible say about that?

When you know – **do what it says; not what you feel, think or even believe**! Do not believe what you want to believe and then try to use the Bible to prove it. Begin with the Bible and conform your beliefs and life to the teachings of the Bible. Please remember it is God who sets the rules; not us. We are only to bind and loose in proper alignment or according to the word of God.

b. **Only make decisions based on the Word or Principles from the WORD**

- **Natural decisions** – use all your senses and consult smart people.
- **Spiritual decisions** – You need a revelation from God about your destiny, for example, getting married or living the single life.

4. **Pray the Word**
   a. Pray **the word**; not your worries.
   b. Pray **the promises of God**; not your problems.
   c. Stand on God's **Promises**; not only on His **Premises**.
   d. **Pray and Believe** according to the Word.
   e. Know when to move from Prayer to Praise.

5. **Instantly obey the promptings of the spirit**
   a. **Delayed obedience** is disobedience
   b. **Partial obedience** is disobedience.
      For example, Saul (1 Sa 15:23).
   c. Know and follow **Intuition** each day.
   d. The Spirit knows, our minds only understand
      - Be led by the spirit … they are the sons of God (Gal 5:16; Rom 8:14).
      - Worship in spirit and truth (Jhn 4:23).
   e. **Always** walk in the spirit (Gal 5:16).

I hope you have grasped the centrality of the word in spiritual training. Your victory and strength will only be realized in and through the Word of God. It is your obedience to the word that set us firm on a rock or the rock (Mat 7:24-27).

PART 8: How to Dress the Human Spirit

In this chapter, I will look at how to protect oneself from the onslaughts of the enemy. Since we are in warfare, God provided a way to be totally protected from all of Satan devices. Satan can't even touch us, if we walk as God intended for his people. John said, "We know that whosoever is born of God sinneth not; but he that is begotten of God keepeth himself, and that wicked one toucheth him not" (1Jn. 5:18). We will discuss Ephesians 6:10-18 briefly on four levels: **Let's read the text slowly, prayerfully, carefully and with more observance than usual.**

> Eph 6:10 Finally, my brethren, **be strong in the Lord**, and in the **power of his might**. 11 Put **on the whole armour of God**, that ye may be able to stand against the **wiles of the devil**. 12 For we wrestle not against flesh and blood, but against principalities, against powers, against the rulers of the darkness of this world, against spiritual wickedness in high *places*. 13 **Wherefore take unto you** the whole armour of God, that ye may be able to withstand in the evil day, and having done all, to stand. 14 Stand therefore, having your loins girt about with **truth**, and having on the breastplate of **righteousness**; 15 And your feet shod with the preparation of the gospel of **peace**; 16

Above all, taking the shield of **faith**, wherewith ye shall be able to quench all the fiery darts of the wicked. 17 And take the helmet of **salvation**, and the sword of the **Spirit**, which is the **word of God**: 18 Praying always with all prayer and supplication in the Spirit, and watching thereunto with all perseverance and supplication for all saints; (**emphasis mine**)

Level One – Basic Approach

At this level, we remove the imagery of helmet, breastplate and so forth. Why I do this is quite simple; ask almost any Christian who studies Ephesians 6 the following questions and note the answers:

1. What is the belt of truth?
2. What is the breastplate of righteousness?
3. What is the preparation of the Gospel of peace?
4. What is the shield of faith?
5. What is the helmet of salvation?
6. What is the sword of the spirit?

The answers you get should be: **truth, righteousness, peace, faith, salvation, spirit.** You will notice one inconsistency in the answers – they will change spirit to Word of God. We are now left with: **truth, righteousness, peace, faith, salvation, in the spirit/in**

the word of God. We recognize that we have spiritual enemies fighting against us daily and consistently. Therefore, as believers, **we should walk in truth, righteousness, peace, faith, salvation, in the spirit/in the word of God**. Do not get distracted with the Roman Soldiers' appearance at the time Paul was writing, that's never God's intent. The armour of God is mentioned in the Old Testament long before there was a Roman Soldier – Paul knew it quite well. For example, the **High Priest's Garments were in fact a spiritual armor**; The High Priest's garments were given to him in order for him to approach God properly in prayer. His main role is to make intercession for himself and the nation. He wore six main things: breastplate, ephod, a robe, coat, mitre, and a girdle. These six correspond very well to the six pieces mentioned in Ephesians 6.

The label should not be used rigidly by us because Paul and Isaiah changed around the terms a little from time to time. For example, in First Thessalonians 5:8, Paul said, "But let us, who are of the day, be sober, putting on the *breastplate of faith and love; and for a helmet, the hope of salvation.*" (Emphasis added) The point is quite clear; the armour protects the child of God who wears it. We will conquer the enemy if we walk in truth, righteousness, peace, faith, salvation, in the spirit/in the word of God. No one can deny or debate away this fact, based on the Word of God, the Bible. If you want to go deeper read the following passages: Exodus 28; Isaiah 11:5, 52:7, 59:17-19, 61:10; First Peter 1:13.

Level Two

At this level, each piece of the armour points to something physical, moral or spiritual that the believer should carefully protect.

Belt of truth to cover our loins. The loin area is where **sexuality and reproduction** must be covered by and with the truth of God's Word. This is in order to remain sexually pure. Too many believers are getting messed up in this area of our walk. The world has no standard in the area of sexuality and in the church we have not yet gotten issues of sexuality under subjection to the Lordship of Christ. **From personal observation, most of those who backslid from the Church, were defiled sexually – even persons who were already married**.

Breastplate of righteousness – this covers the chest, which covers the heart. Proverbs 4:22 said, "Keep thy heart with all diligence; for out of it *are* the issues of life." Another word for keep is guard. Guard your heart. Keep it clean and pure. God wants clean hands and pure hearts to ascend his holy hill. I have heard it said that, "the heart of the matter, is the matter of the heart." This point cannot be over emphasized.

Feet shod with the preparation of the gospel of peace – our Lord is the Prince of Peace. Our feet should not be swift or involved in running into mischief (Pro 1:16). We live and carry a message of peace to all men. Peace is listed under the fruit of the spirit. The ultimate peace of the gospel is peace with God himself (Rom 5:1).

The shield of faith – This help cover the **entire body**. Redemption in its fullness, protects our bodies – the temple of the Holy Spirit (1Co 3:16-17). Our bodies are very important to God, they shall be changed at the coming of our Lord Jesus Christ (1 Th 4:16-18). We were saved by grace through faith (Eph 2:8). The just shall live by faith (Heb 10:38). We walk by faith not by sight (2 Co 5:7). We can't please God without faith (Heb 11:6).

The helmet of salvation – the helmet cover the head. **The head host the five sense organs**. Seeing, hearing, smelling, tasting and feelings (face covers with a portion of skin) are all operated from the head. **The head, most of all, host the Brain**. The Brain is the physical part; but the mind is about its operation intellectually. The Brain controls the body; but the mind controls the entire function of the man as it relate to God, himself and his environment. The mind is the battlefield where we pull down strongholds, hear God's Word and apply it to our personal walk with God (1 Co 10:3-5). The mind MUST be renewed in order to walk in the spirit and have a life of total victory. The Holy Spirit speaks to our spirits and the spirit conveys or reveals what God spoke or impressed on the spirit. The mind then process and should follow God's directions in the Power of the Holy Spirit. This area alone could become a book by itself because of the vastness of its significance. *There are two totally opposite mindsets at war in the believer- that of God and Satan* (2 Co 10:3-5).

The sword of the Spirit, which is the word of God: The sword is the only OFFENSIVE part of the armour. The other parts of the armour protect and defend us against the enemy's assaults on us. The sword is what can deal a death blow to the works of the enemy and send the enemy wounded or defeated. Jesus did exactly this when he was tempted by the

Devil. Jesus spoke ONLY the Word against the Devil. The phrase, "which is the word of God" is very important, hence, I will go just one more step deeper. The Greek word used for "word" is "rhema." "Rhema" is God's spoken word. It is what God is speaking or saying to you in a specific way and time. It is God's NOW WORD to us or speaking the written word under divine unction by faith. **Rhema is never used for what we now called the Bible or that which is written**. The Greek word used for that which is written is *"graphe."* *"Graphe"* is the word primarily used for the Bible, which means scripture. Rarely, if ever, is either of the words translated "word" (*"logos"* or *"rhema"*) used for the Bible. We are well aware that it was the *"logos"* that became flesh and dwelt among us (Joh 1:14). (See the glossary for a complete listing and translation of the words: *"logos," "rhema," "graphe"* and *"grapho."*) So be very careful lest you believe because you have or carry a Bible you are fully armed. A Bible you (or others carry); but don't read, study or meditate on. A Bible you don't know what is written in it, neither are you speaking its message. (Jos 1:8)

Praying always with all prayer and supplication in the Spirit – All of the armor is operated by or through prayer. Verse 18 in Greek begins with the preposition "dia" from which we get the English word diameter. Strong's said, "A primary preposition denoting the *channel* of an act; *through....* the ground or reason by which something is or is not done." The verse should start with one of the followings ways: through all prayer, by all prayer or by the means of all prayer. The armor is maintained and kept active through prayer. Jesus said "men aught always to pray and not to faint. (Luk 18:1) Paul knew this secret as he wrote his epistles to believers. He wrote in Philippians 4:6, "Be careful for nothing; but in everything by prayer and supplication with thanksgiving let your requests be made known unto God." First Thessalonians 5:17, "Pray without ceasing."

Level Three

At this level, I will outline some **principles** concerning the **armor of God**.

1. God provides the armour for us; but we should put it on. He will not do it for us.
2. We need the armour to stand and withstand the enemy.
3. There is an armour for each believer.
4. God spoke clearly in my spirit, "IT IS GOD'S ARMOUR; NOT OURS." GOD WEARS THIS

ARMOUR HIMSELF. Guzik confirmed this word when he wrote, "This armor is **of God** both in the sense that it is from Him, and in the sense that it *is His actual armor*. In the Old Testament, it is the LORD who wears the armor (Isa 59:17). He now shares that armor with us - no wonder we are *more than conquerors*! (Rom 8:37)" (Guzik Commentary)

5. God makes available to us what he used in battle. **Exodus 15:3** declared, "The LORD *is* a man of war: the LORD *is* his name" and **"Jehovah Gibbor Milchamah" - The LORD Mighty in Battle (Psa 24:8).** Isaiah 59:17 For he (The LORD) put on righteousness as a breastplate, and a helmet of salvation upon his head; and he put on the garments of vengeance *for* clothing, and was clad with zeal as a cloke.

6. The armour of God looks the same on each of us – the enemy doesn't know who exactly he is fighting in the spirit. He/They sees a whole army or body of soldiers/saints looking exactly like God. He can't be certain if it is the Angel of the LORD, Angels or human spirit dressed in God's armour. He cannot fight God and win, so he has to flee when he is resisted (Jas 4:7).

Level Four

We have established that it is God's armour at this point. I will now take a deeper look at the armour. It will give further clarity to level three. We will now look at the armour as *an armour of light.*

The armour of God is bright, too much for the eye to gaze upon. Demons can't handle true light that comes from God. Let us look briefly on who God is. **God is light**. "This then is the message which we have heard of him, and declare unto you, that **God is light**, and in him is no darkness at all." (1Jhn 1:5) Psalm 84:11 "For the LORD God *is* a **sun and shield**: the LORD will give grace and glory: no good *thing* will he withhold from them that walk uprightly."

God is covered in and with light. Psalm 104:2 states, "Who coverest *thyself* with **light** as *with* a garment: who stretchest out the heavens like a curtain." Psalm 27:1, "The LORD *is* my **light and my salvation**; whom shall I fear? The LORD *is* the strength of my life; of whom shall I be afraid?"

God raise us up in Christ who is light. Romans 13:14 "But put ye on the Lord Jesus Christ, and make not provision for the flesh, to *fulfill* the lusts *thereof.*" John

8:12 "Then spake Jesus again unto them, saying, I am the **light** of the world: he that followeth me shall not walk in darkness, but shall have the **light** of life."

We are now patterned after Christ. Ephesians 5:8 "For ye were sometimes darkness, but **now** *are ye* **light in the Lord**: walk as children of light." Believers were called the light of the world by Jesus himself. Jesus said, "Ye are the light of the world. A city that is set on a hill cannot be hid" (Mat 5:14). Psalm 37:6 "and he shall bring forth thy righteousness as the **light**, and thy judgment as the noonday."

We too are light in life - Romans 13:12 "The night is far spent, the day is at hand: let us therefore cast off the works of darkness, and let us put on the **armour of light**.

Key Revelation-Knowledge about the armour

I am about to share something with you that I heard once from a servant of God. I became doubtful and ignored it as something that sound impossible until the Lord took me on the battlefield, in the realm of the spirit. Here is the revelation; *There is a place in the realm of the spirit where Satan and demons can't see you; but you can see them.* Please read the following two verses and take note of the *Robe of Righteousness*:

> We know that whosoever is born of God sinneth not; but he that is begotten of God keepeth himself, and that wicked one toucheth him not (1Jn 5:18).

> I will greatly rejoice in the LORD, my soul shall be joyful in my God; for he hath clothed me with the garments of salvation, *he hath covered me with the robe of righteousness*, as a bridegroom decketh himself with ornaments, and as a bride adorneth herself with her jewels (Isa 61:10) (Emphasis added).

Every Christian should strive to live holy. I am not talking about being self-righteous. I am talking about honoring the righteousness of Christ in us. Living holy is not just a hell or heaven issue; it is the key to our victory in this present world. I found myself at a place in the realm of the spirit and all of a sudden I saw a whole army of soldiers and tankers coming in my direction. They had guns of all types, especially those that could fire a whole lot of live rounds per minute. As I stood there watching and wondering, they started firing directly at me. They came to kill me that day. I started to run and fly in the realm of the spirit – really fast. But no matter how fast I moved, I could not out run or out fly them. So I decided in my heart that I will not run anymore; but stop and fight this army to the death. Immediately the heavens were opened and a **white robe** came down to me and I put it on in a few seconds. By the time I put on the robe they were already where I was standing. It was then I realized they could not see me – the robe made me invisible to them. I stood there beside them – hearing and seeing them. They started arguing in amazement with each other, saying, *"Where is he, he was just standing right here."* There was something else that happened; I am certain they did not miss when they were firing at me; but the armour protected me from every bullet (Paul said fiery darts). I share this to encourage each believer to walk in the spirit and we will continue to be an overcomer through Jesus Christ our Lord. We should also understand the gifts of the Spirit, which we will do in the next chapter.

PART 9: Gifts of the Holy Spirit I Corinthians 12:1–11

Throughout the Old and New Testaments God blessed his people with several gifts in all areas of life and leadership. Hence I am making it clear that I am not attempting to list and explain all the gifts God gives to his church. I am only looking on the nine mentioned in I Corinthians **12:1–11.** You can read Romans 12 and Ephesians 4 for further discussions on the same subject matter. Paul did not want the Corinthians to be ignorant concerning spiritual gifts or matters of faith.

Paul said the Holy Spirit exalts Jesus as Lord and all those who have the Holy Spirit will do the same: He said there are:

Diversities of **Gifts**   same **Spirit** v 4

Diversities of **operations**   same **Lord**

Differences of **administrations**   same **God**

Please note it is the Manifestations of the Spirit; not us or God's servants. All the credits should go to God; not man.

The gifts are given to every man to profit (benefit) withal (v. 7, 11). The gifts are given, not for the honor and glory of the one who receives the gifts; but for the edifying of the Body of Christ, the Church. Not using ones gifts causes the whole body to suffer lack or need. To say it bluntly, "it is a sin against God and the Body of Christ not to use one's gifts."

Now, everyone has natural abilities from birth; but only believers have spiritual gifts given them at or subsequent to conversion. The Holy Spirit decides which gift(s) one receives. This does not exclude us from requesting, through prayer, other gifts. E.g. Paul said all who speak in tongues should pray to interpret. Each gift is discussed or describe below under three headings:

Power to Know – Revelation Gifts

Word of Wisdom – information and direction from God, Wisdom is the Ability to recognize difference. As a result, accurate choices can be made.

Word of Knowledge (Greek – "*gnōsis*") – information from God you could never get any other way.

Discernment of Spirits – not just demons; but human spirits as well. The **Purpose of the gift of discernment is** to establish the **source** and not the

Results of activities (healing, miracles, prophecy, and tongues). Source is what determines real from counterfeit.

NOTE – Authenticity is measured by the SOURCE of the operation; not the RESULTS themselves.

Power to Do – Power Gifts

Faith – unusual endowment to believe God. Faith removes mountains. All things are possible with God and to him that believes (Mar 9:23; 10:27).

F.A.I.T.H. – **F**ull **A**ssurance **I**n **T**he **H**eart that gives **F**ull **A**ccess **I**nto **T**he **H**eavens

Gifts of Healings – Please note both words are plural. Healing physically, emotionally and Spiritual. Restoring wholeness to individuals by the power of God.

Gifts of Miracles (dunamis) – Please note both words are plural. Miracles defy nature. Miracles flow more on the creative side, more than the restorative side.

Power to Say – Vocal Gifts

There is a misunderstanding among some Pentecostals in this area. Once a person speaks in tongues regularly we assume the person has or is exercising the gift of tongues. However, there are **two categories of Tongues (languages):**

Devotional tongues – mainly personal and private; but may still be interpreted. It is man talking to God with his spirit. Human spirit to the Spirit of God. The believers have control over this type of tongues. Discuss mainly in First Corinthians 14:14-15. The Purposes:

- To flow with the Holy Spirit.
- Build us up.
- Strengthens our faith.
- Keep us in love (Jud 20-21).
- Speak directly to God (I Co 14:2).
- To speak mysteries with his or her spirit.

Diverse Kinds of tongues – This gift operates **mainly in Public or Corporate Gatherings of the believers. It is God speaking to His people through an individual; hence interpretation comes with this type of tongues through the same person or someone else in the audience or congregation, so that all may be edified.** In order for everything to go well Paul encouraged such person to pray to interpret because someone can disobey God and not give the interpretation. This gift can:

- Build up the atmosphere of worship.
- Revolutionize our communities or cities as in Acts 2 AND
- ALWAYS COMES WITH AN **INTERPRETATION.**

It is this gift Paul mentioned in chapter twelve of first Corinthians, verse thirty, "Have all the gifts of healing? Do all speak with tongues? Do all interpret?" His rhetorical questions carry a **NO** for each answer. This is so because these gifts were exercised by some believers, as the Spirit deemed fitting or based on how receptive and open to God an individual was at that point in time when God wishes to send a word to His people.

Interpretation of Tongues – not a translation.

- It is a summary or meaning of what was said in kinds or diverse tongues.
- It may be given to the speaker or another person in the audience.
- It is to edify the Congregation as a group.
- When interpretation is given, it is now called a **Prophecy.**
- **An interpreter can pick up Satanic utterances if persons come to curse the church or if they are demonized.**

Prophecy – To speak forth the mind and will of God. There are three types of prophets that can be found in scripture

- **"Chosem"** (used for a **false prophet**) – they can deliver a true word like Balaam.
- **"Navi" Level I** – Navi means to Bubble up, spring of water. This prophet received mainly words; not pictures, from God in order to prophesy.
- **"Ro'eh" level II** – seer, receive words and pictures. This individual is usually given spiritual secrets and keys in the realm of the spirit like Samuel.

Let us continue to seek God and use the gifts he bestowed upon us for his glory. Gifts show forth the power and goodness of God in the midst of his people to mend the hurting and guide us supernaturally. When you learn the gifts, let us now see how they relate to the fruit of the spirit.

PART 10: The Gifts Versus the Fruit of the Spirit

One night, during a prayer meeting at church, I was very saddened when God used an individual to bring a word of prophecy. The individual was the one with a lot of obvious flaws and bad attitudes. So I would rather God used someone else at that given moment of time. There and then the Lord comforted me with these words, "**We serve a Perfect God, who use imperfect people to do His perfect will**." As the Pastor, I realized God can use any one to do His will even though we all have flaws and immature tendencies. God gave me greater clarity between Gifts and fruit of the Spirit. That same night the Holy Spirit spoke these words to me, **"The gifts can take you to Heavenly Places; but they can't keep you there. They can make you prominent and well sought after by many. The fruit keep you where the gifts take you. Without fruit you will become a public disgrace because you will fall for a lack of the fruit of the spirit."**

Here are some of the points to ponder. The table in figure one will make things clearer and easier to detect a believer level of maturity.

Figure 1

SPIRITUAL GIFTS	FRUIT OF THE SPIRIT
Gifts (Plural)	Fruit (Singular)
Gifts – are unearned, came from God at His Will. Maybe be requested by the believer. Can have an immediate impact in the Body of Christ	Fruit – implies roots and growth which takes time to cultivate. It is the believer's responsibility to bear the fruit.
Need to be exercised and developed	Need to be exercised and developed
Has nothing to do with who are mature	Show who are mature in the faith
Show God's power	Show God's Character or attributes
Signs of Ministry	Signs of Maturity
More for the Body's Growth	More for the believer's growth
The gifts can take you to Heavenly Places; but they can't keep you there. Can make you prominent and well sought after by many	**The fruit keep you where the gifts take you. Without fruit you will become a public disgrace because you will fall**
Gifts can still operate without fruit(1Co13:1-2)	By their fruit you shall know them
They are Primarily for Here and Now	They will be going with us into Eternity

Another thing God impressed on my spirit was this. Whenever a man or woman of God get into disgrace or scandal, he was warned at least twice and did not repent or take heed. God practices his own word, Matthew 18:15–16 reads, "Moreover if thy brother shall trespass against thee, go and tell him his fault between thee and him alone: if he shall hear thee, thou hast gained thy brother. But if he will not hear *thee, then* take with thee one or two more, that in the mouth of two or three witnesses every word may be established." Principles: Sins are trespasses against God. So God warned such a person personally, then through one, two or three witnesses. It may be through a preached word, dream or vision.

Here is another **SERIOUS MATTER TO WATCH AND BE WARNED ABOUT as a believer**. I was watching a well beloved man of God on television teaching on the gifts of the Spirit and qualifications for God to use an individual. Here is what he said, *"God cannot use you if you are not walking or living a holy life."* I understood what he said, but felt sickly uneasy on my inside, my spirit was very disturbed because millions were listening all across the world. Pastor what was your problem you may ask. Let me explain what the Holy Ghost gave me on the issue.

Gifts can still operate without fruit. Paul said, "Though I speak with the tongues of men and of angels, and have not charity, I am become as sounding brass, or a tinkling cymbal. And though I have the gift of prophecy, and understand all mysteries, and all knowledge; and though I have all faith, so that I could remove mountains, and have not charity, I am nothing (1Co 13:1-2). The gifts working does not mean the lifestyle of the person is approved by God (like Samson). Ministers who are committing adultery; fornication; lying; and stealing may enter the pulpit; and preach, and the people will get blessed; healed; and signs and wonders will take place. They felt okay because God used them. *"God cannot use you if you are not walking or living a holy life"* therefore my adultery must be okay or God wouldn't use me so mightily. This notion is a lie from the pit of hell. It is a master deception that some ministers have accepted. A scandal may be God's way of rescuing such a person from total destruction. It's not all Satan's doing, trust me on this one! Yes - the devil and evil people may mock the church; but God is at work to warn others who are on a similar path. Don't give the devil all the blame or credit my friends. I used to blame him until the Lord gave me insight into the matter.

Here are a few more comments on the fruit of the spirit directly. Galatians 5:22 **"But the fruit of the Spirit is love, joy, peace, longsuffering, gentleness, goodness, faith, 23 Meekness, temperance: against such there is no law."** A critical question we should answer before we go further is, **"Which spirit is Paul referring to in this chapter generally and in these two verses in particular: the Holy Spirit or the Born Again Human Spirit?"** If you examine chapter five carefully and other passages prayerfully and carefully, you will conclude that Paul was referring to the Born Again Human Spirit. Jesus said concerning false prophets, "Ye shall know them by their fruits...." **(Mat 7:16)** We will show forth our fruit based on who we are on the inside. Those who know God will reflect godly character in their lives. The Holy Spirit is not the one bearing the fruit; he is the one enabling us to bear godly fruit in our lives through our submission to him. If it was the Holy Spirit, ALL believers would possess ALL the fruit listed in proper balance - the Holy Spirit could not and would not fail to produce. Jesus said, "I am the vine, ye *are* the branches: He that abideth in me, and I in him, the same bringeth forth much fruit: for without me ye can do nothing. Fruit bear on the branches – us the believers (Jhn 15:5). He (Jesus) said

the same (the believer) bringeth forth much fruit; by and through his strength and supply, of course, through our abiding in Him. Let us now take a closer look at each of the nine fruit of the spirit.

1. **Love (agape)** - we begin to learn true love and how to express it in a godly way. We grow in love as we grow in God, because God is love.
2. **Joy** – inward delight that is not dependent of circumstances. God is the person of our joy.
3. **Peace** – from Shalom, peace, quietness, rest. Shalom is a complete word that covers all areas of prosperity. True prosperity starts on the inside of the believer. Our souls must be prospering in God and then reflect in material things in persons lives.
4. **Patience/Longsuffering** – this is to be able to rest confidently in God in difficult times. One wait without murmuring and complaining – it is the quality of waiting and not just spending time.
5. **Gentleness** - *usefulness*, moral *excellence*, gentleness, goodness.
6. **Goodness** - virtue or beneficence, we once again start to manifest true actions that please God.
7. **Faith** – faithfulness, stable, reliable.
8. **Meekness** – gentle, humble and mild in demeanor. Meekness is not weakness. Weakness

is the absence of strength; but meekness is strength under control.

9. **Self-control** – this is to be able to master yourself. The first person to conquer in this world is you. Master yourself, master your life. You are now usable to God and His work. If God can't restrain you he can't send you.

Let us seek to develop the character of God in us – fruit of the spirit and not just seek to be in the performance line – gifts of the Spirit. God wants to see himself in us, more than how he wants to work through us. For example, Concerning Jesus Christ, God said he was well pleased with him before he started to perform his ministry of signs and wonders.

PART 11: Understanding Spiritual Authority

All that you have learnt so far about Spiritual Growth, Laws of the Spirit, How to Train the Human Spirit, How to Dress the Human Spirit, Gifts of the Holy Spirit, The Gifts of the Holy Spirit versus the Fruit of the Spirit amongst other thing, MUST ALL BE DONE WITHIN GOD'S ESTABLISH AUTHORITY. As a result I must include some principles that govern how God's Kingdom operates. We will begin with the following verse:

> Romans 13:1–2. Let every soul be subject unto the higher **powers**. For there is no **power** but of God: the **powers** that be are ordained of God. Whosoever therefore resisteth the **power** resisteth the ordinance of God: and they that resist shall receive to themselves damnation (Emphasis added).

> Matthew 28:18 And Jesus came and spake unto them, saying, All **power** is given unto me in heaven and in earth. (Emphasis added)

> Luke 10:19 Behold, I give unto you **power** to tread on serpents and scorpions, and over all the **power** of the enemy: and nothing shall by any means hurt you. (Emphasis added)

Acts 1:8 But ye shall receive **power**, after that the Holy Ghost is come upon you: and ye shall be witnesses unto me both in Jerusalem, and in all Judaea, and in Samaria, and unto the uttermost part of the earth. (Emphasis added)

Concepts to Remember

Please read over the passages above and take note of the word "**power**" which I placed emphasis on. The word power in the above passages translated two different Greek words. These two Greek words have different emphases and implications we should note.

1. "ἐξουσία" (*exousia*) - this word is better translated as Authority. **Authority is the RIGHT TO DO SOMETHING** in a specific sphere, realm, domain, territory, such as: rule, act, or control among others. This must be conveyed on an individual.

2. "δύναμις" (*dunamis*) – "*Dunamis*" emphasizes **the ABILITY TO DO SOMETHING** in a specific sphere, realm, domain, territory, such as: rule, act, or control among others. This is usually inherent or learnt over time through training or practice.

In **Romans** the word exousia (authority) is used by Paul in both verses. Paul was addressing legitimate authority in the world in his day and by extension today. Our study focus will be the church and how God intends believers to submit to and exercise authority. In **Matthew** the word exousia was used by Jesus to his disciples – he had all **authority** in heaven and in earth. In **Luke** both words were used by Jesus, "power (exousia) authority to tread...all the power (dunamis) ability of the enemy." Acts 1: 8 used dunamis to describe what the disciples would receive days later on the Day of Pentecost in Acts chapter two and onwards.

Let me illustrate how the two words, are to be understood for the most part. Police officers in Jamaica have authority or **the right to do** things under the laws of Jamaica. The officer on duty, for example, may stop a vehicle and ask the driver for his documents and licence. If the driver has no licence to drive – he may **have the ability to drive; but not the right to drive** and therefore would be fined. To lawfully drive on the road, an individual needs the right (*"exousia"* or licence) to drive and the ability (dunamis) to drive. Both are needed at all times to be lawful. A Jamaican police who travel overseas looses the right to exercise the same functions because his authority is limited to Jamaican territory. Let me take this concept deeper for our study purposes. In the church we have two categories of authority:

1. **Positional Authority** – filled in various ways based on the denomination or group, such as appointment by a person or committee, elected by majority vote. **A usurper is satanic.** A usurper seeks to seize and hold a position, office, power by force or without legal right. They take authority without being elected or appointed by legitimate or established authority.

2. **Spiritual Authority** – this is rooted in understanding of the Word and Will of God. **Your level of Spiritual Authority is determined by how well you know God's Word and God's Will and are walking in obedience to the same.** God's Words embodies his authority, so a lack of understanding of the Word automatically limits your spiritual authority. Only those who know **God's Words and God's Will** can speak and represent him in the Kingdom.

Watchman Nee said, "The acts of God issue from His throne and His throne is established on His authority.

All things are created through God's authority and all physical laws of the universe are maintained by His authority." He went further by saying, "God's authority represents God himself whereas His power stands only for His act." (Nee 1972, p. 10)

To serve God's church or people lawfully an individual needs two things:

1. **Be Anointed** – The Anointing is the Dunamis or Ability to do God's will
2. **Be Appointed** – Those you want to serve or called to serve, MUST APPROVE YOU - **exousia**.

Here are some ministry twins that should not be separated, under no circumstances, one must follow the other and not be in reverse. **Spiritual authority** MUST be followed by **positional authority** – DO NOT REVERSE. I am not saying we should find or make positions for persons who have spiritual authority. What I am saying is this, if a vacancy arises for a position of authority, look for the spiritual authority in the individual before you make the appointment. This leads to my next twin: **Anointing and Appointing.** **Anointing** MUST be followed by the "**Appointing**" - DO NOT REVERSE. Look for the Anointing in an individual's life before you appoint him to a task or responsibility. Remember the Anointing is the ABILITY TO DO something and the Appointment is the AUTHORITY TO DO it.

Church leaders MUST understand these concepts in order to lead God's people correctly. A position or an appointment CANNOT give the individual anointing and spiritual authority. Leaders without spiritual authority can kill the ministry and stifle the life of the believers. Without spiritual authority that is equal to or above the position of authority, the leader will become proud and self conceited. If the leader is too small for the position of authority he or she will act and speak like Nebuchadnezzar. "The king spake, and said, Is not this great Babylon, that I have built for the house of the kingdom by the might of my power, and for the honor of my majesty?" (Dan 4:30) Bishop T. D. Jakes said something I will never forget. He said, "If you are too big for a small church; you are too small for a big church." He also said, "As long as the ministry does not outgrow the minister everything is alright. The minister must remain bigger than the ministry." Pastors who only study theology at a Bible school without being converted, saved, born again cannot advance God's work. They can do mental and theoretical work, but are unable to impart spiritual life. It is the spirit, Jesus said, that gives life. Everything produces according to its kind (Gen 1:11). This is one of the reasons why over time congregations grow into the image of the pastor or leader. A person or disciple can only reproduce who he is, nothing else.

Five types of leaders in churches

1. **The Anointed and Appointed (King Saul before** he was rejected by God-1 Sam. 10). This is God's model for his people. It is God who calls and anoints people for ministry; but he appoints through people. God appoints **through** his established leaders within the Body of Christ or local church. "In serving God we must not violate authorities, because to do so is a principle of Satan. How can we preach Christ according to Satan's principle? Yet it is possible in our work to stand with Christ in doctrine while at the same time stand with Satan in principle.... Never should we who serve God serve according to the principle of Satan. Whenever the principle according to Christ is operating, that of Satan fades away." (Nee 1972, p. 11)

2. **The Anointed; but not Appointed (David** 1Sam 16:13-14) When David was anointed to be king, Saul was still the ruling king. David had to wait over twenty years before he was appointed as king. Too

many persons with an anointing on their lives can't wait on God. They believe they must be appointed immediately to some special position. Some undermined leadership and others just leave and start a ministry of their own. Some even split the ministry and take some persons with them to their new work. "Let us know that there are two principles in the universe: the principle of God's authority and the principle of Satanic rebellion. We cannot serve God and simultaneously go the way of rebellion by having a rebellious spirit. Satan laughs when a rebellious person preaches the word, for in that person is dwelling the Satanic principle. The principle of service must be authority. Are we going to obey God's authority or not? We who serve God must have this basic understanding of authority." (Nee 1972, pp. 16-17)

3. **The Appointed; but not Anointed** (**Saul after** he was rejected by God 1Sam 16:14). Saul remained in his appointed position as king; yet he was no longer anointed as a king. The Spirit of God departed from him to David. As a result he tried hard to kill David for over twenty years. Saul disqualified himself. David did not run for Saul's office or tried to get support or enough signatures or votes. Leaders who are disqualified will always fight against anyone

around him with God's favor or gifting to function in his office. Insecurity trips in and all perceived threats must be cast out. Hence a power struggle develops in leadership that can end tragically, as it did with Saul who died disgracefully.

4. **The Anointed; but Self Appointed** (**Lucifer** Isa 14:12-15; Eze 28:11-17) Lucifer was the anointed Cherub; but he wanted a position liken to that of God. He exalted himself and was cast out of heaven. **Self-exaltation** is a **Luciferian principle.** He wanted a position that belonged to God alone. He wanted a position not assigned to him or he was not appointed to such a position. He tried to usurp God's Authority. **To usurp authority** is another Luciferian Principle. *Lucifer is behind every church split. Lucifer split the first church and he still does the same today.* "Should the principle on which we work and serve include rebellion, then Satan will obtain and enjoy glory even through our sacrifices." (Nee 1972, p. 15) He was anointed for his assignment; but chose to leave his place of assignment. Every believer needs to know his place of assignment. Stay within your scope of anointing at all times. Are you anointed for local, district, parish, national, regional or an inter-national or global ministry? If you are anointed for your congregation only – stay there. To go beyond that is

self exaltation, to usurp authority or to take upon you a position not assigned by God. In this case, God will not back a usurper – it is a Luciferian principle.

5. **The Self-Appointed; but not Anointed (Absalom 2 Sa 15–18)** Absalom stole the heart of the people from David. In battle he was caught by his own locks, suspended between heaven and earth (2 Sa 18:9) His mule went out from under him leaving him hanging by his own locks. This is what will be the fate of all self-appointed and not anointed leader. They shall die by their own craft or head or counsel. So will be their Ahithophel who give advice against God's anointed and appointed leaders. "Any attempt to set up oneself as an authority must be totally eradicated from among us. Let God establish His authority; let no man ever try. Should God really appoint you to be an authority, you have two alternatives before you: either you disobey and recede spiritually or you obey and receive grace." (Nee 1972, p. 122)

A Word to Pastors

God will not give insights and wisdom to a pastor just because he/she is in the position of pastor. The pastor has to pray, study and seek God's face like any other member. Or else a member who does so will grow and reach a higher level of spiritual authority above that of the pastor. The pastor remains the appointed head of the flock; but operates below members according to spiritual authority. In some churches, members have been walking with God before the pastor was born. They are stable, wise, mature and spiritually discerning. Such persons earned the right to be respected as an Elder of the church. A pastor must understand the privilege of being called and appointed to provide covering and guidance to such individuals because it's all by the grace of God. In a natural family, the child who was born first assume or is given authority over all the others as the eldest one or the first born (born first). He who got saved first has authority over the others except where gifting, callings and spiritual growth places the younger above the older. This happens also because spiritual growth is not time bound as natural birth. Time is important in all things; but must only be used where spiritual maturity is present to support the same. I have met quite a few persons who can boast of being around for over thirty or more year in the faith. But they lack basic bible knowledge, a good temperament and problem solving skills.

A pastor has to be careful to keep ahead in spiritual things above his congregants. The pastor is the person of theology that is properly grounded in the WORD. The pastor must not be distracted by those who are excelling in other fields of endeavor. A pastor of a church with a lot of highly qualified professionals need not be intimidated to go and earn a degree in the other fields of endeavor to feel on par. This is why some are preaching and teaching psychology and philosophy instead of theology – may God help us. As a pastor, learn all you can; but be committed to keep the main thing, the main thing. Everyone needs a pastor, so the pastor doesn't need to be like everybody else. Always keep your difference and keep spiritually sharp.

PART 12: The Word Made Flesh Today

The Word made flesh is not a second or third incarnation like that of Jesus Christ. Instead, it is the Word of God becoming our daily lifestyle. It is the Word of God becoming our habits and practices in all areas of our life. It is how we embody the word of God today as the body of Christ.

> **John 1:14** And the Word was made flesh, and dwelt among us, (and we beheld his glory, the glory as of the only begotten of the Father,) full of grace and truth.

> **Romans 6:20** For when ye were the servants of sin, ye were free from righteousness....22 But now being made free from sin, and become servants to God, ye have your fruit unto holiness, and the end everlasting life.

> **Galatians 4:19** My little children, of whom I travail in birth again until Christ be formed in you

> **1John 3:6** Whosoever abideth in him sinneth not: whosoever sinneth hath not seen him, neither known him. 7 Little children, let no man deceive you: he that doeth righteousness is righteous, even as he is righteous. 8 He that committeth sin is of the devil; for the devil sinneth from the beginning. For this purpose the Son of God was manifested, that he might destroy the

works of the devil. 9 Whosoever is born of God doth not commit sin; for his seed remaineth in him: and he cannot sin, because he is born of God.

Gal 5:16 *This* I say then, Walk in the Spirit, and ye shall not fulfil the lust of the flesh.

Dr Cindy Trimm said if you do something for thirty (30) days, its discipline. Do it for sixty (60) days, it's a habit. Do it for ninety (90) days and it becomes a lifestyle. After hearing one (1) lie, we will need to hear the truth at least thirteen (13) times to reverse that lie.

A changed life means things I usually do, I CAN'T DO ANY MORE. IN SIN - **wrong was easy, while Right was hard** or took great effort. IN RIGHTEOUSNESS - Right should now be easy as a believer while sin is hard or takes great effort to do – the new or divine nature won't permit or allow sin to reign. The Holy Spirit spoke to my heart and lifted my spirit one day concerning us as believers. He said, **"UNBELIEVERS FIND IT DIFFICULT TO LIVE RIGHT BECAUSE THEY HAVE THE OLD SINFUL NATURE. ON THE OTHER HAND, BELIEVERS WITH A NEW NATURE SHOULD NOW FIND IT DIFFICULT TO SIN. THERE IS A PLACE IN ME THAT WILL MAKE SINNING DIFFICULT AND**

LIVING RIGHT NORMAL." Believe me; if you live right consistently, right living will become your DISCIPLINE, then your HABIT, then your LIFESTYLE. According to Galatians 5: 16, IF we walk in the Spirit, it will be **IMPOSSIBLE** (in Greek it is in the **DOUBLE NEGATIVE, DEPICTING THE IMPOSSIBLE**) **TO FULFILL THE LUST OF THE FLESH**. We cannot walk in the flesh and the Spirit simultaneously. We cannot be **in the Spirit** and **SINNING** at the same time. In 1 John above, the word seed in Greek is sperm. We were born from God's sperm or DNA – what a powerful reality. I wish I had the time to expound the verses line by line. Do not make excuse for any sinful habit in your life at the moment. If you do, Satan will use your excuse to keep you bound. Keep you from enjoying the King and the Kingdom.

PART 13: The King and Kingdom Principles

This chapter will cover Understanding the King and the Kingdom, The most important law on earth, and Managing Friendships and relationships. In this section I am heavily indebted to Rabbi Ralph Messer _ I listened to his ministry online at Simchat Torah Beit Midrash (www.torah.tv), on YouTube and here in Jamaica live. I cannot point to any one place or time for the information recorded here. I have been learning from him for years not in order to write this book or else I would have noted dates, times and places to give him proper credit. His teachings are combined with my personal discoveries and learning over many years.

Jesus Christ the Personal Word of God made flesh. He told his followers that Moses in particular wrote about him. The Torah was not given to give salvation or redemption. The Israelites were already saved and redeemed by God from Egypt and Pharaoh. The Torah or Law for some, was given to a redeemed people to learn how to live out a redeemed lifestyle. Each book has imbedded in it principles to live by on a daily basis. The principles of the Torah were given to usher them into a life of blessing and prosperity through their obedience. Deuteronomy twenty eight explains this concept in details. An overview will now show you the bigger picture behind each book of the Torah.

- Overview of Torah (Genesis to Deuteronomy) – laying the foundation for the study
- **5 Steps or Principles of Torah** based in Genesis, Exodus, Leviticus, Numbers and Deuteronomy.

Step 1- Faith (Gen 15:6). Faith (Emunah) deals with the **Unseen Realm Only**. YHWH – Name of God in the Unseen Realm. Faith MUST be attached to **Torah Principles** to be true faith. It does not operate in a vacuum.

Step 2 – Principles (Exo 20) – 613 in all. Called Protocol or Kingdom Order (Legal Positions). **The power to bind – disallow or forbid and loose – allow or permit**. The Laws of God is what determines what things we can bind and loose. It is not left for us to determine. In a kingdom, the king sets and enforces the laws as the sovereign ruler of his domain.

Step 3 – Purpose (Lev 8–10). Applied Principles brings Purpose into view. Plans may change; but Purpose (Torah) is constant. Purpose gives meaning; meaning gives motivation and energy to fight.

Step 4 – Vision (Num 5, 10, 15) always corporate. Three key principles:

I. Whatever you say out of your mouth comes towards you.

II. Whatever you hear, you will repeat (even gossip)

III. Whatever you write down will come to past (Rabbi Ralph Messer) (number your days Psalm 90: 12)

Step 5 – Increase (Deu 28-29) – God will multiply or enlarge us if we get the order and principles correct.

Below is a comparison between the king and the kingdom principles. We often mix up the two and wonder why we are not blessed or prospering as we desire. Bear in mind what Jesus said as you examine your life against the chart below. Jesus said, "And why call ye me, Lord, Lord, and do not the things which I say? (Luk 6:46) and "If ye love me, keep my commandments" (Joh 14:15).

THE PERSON (YESHUA – JESUS) – THE KING	THE PRINCIPLES (TORAH) of JESUS KINGDOM CONSTITUTION/ PROTOCOL
King – Yeshua (Jesus)	Torah – Principles of the Kingdom
Gives us Life to a state (Jhn. 1:4)	Gives us a Lifestyle (that will be made permanent)
He gave the Torah(Law) James 4:12 one lawgiver who is able to save	Reflect the giver's desire
Yeshua creates our Peace	Principles (torah) creates our Prosperity
Yeshua gives us an Experience of God	Principles – gives us the Expertise of God
Yeshua prepares us for Eternity (Heaven), our country (Salvation)	Principles Prepares us for Earth – NOW (Place of dominion) Redemption – taking back territory
Yeshua said Follow ME – Worship Him, Follow God; not a System	Principles – Practice them by faith and Honor, Change your seasons
Yeshua- Show & Help us to Change, Gives us the	Principles – show us what and where we

ability to change	need to change. Command us to change
Yeshua – Sets or Promotes us above Principalities and Powers and so forth	Principles – Bind Principalities and Powers. A Principle always wins over Principalities.
Yeshua – Determines our confidence / Confession	Principles – Determines our Conduct/Walk

PART 14: The Law of Honor

Honor – is the willingness to reward someone for his/her difference. It is the MOST IMPORTANT LAW ON EARTH. Every SIN on earth is a sin of Dishonor (to God or Man). It is not an anointing, a miracle, not an answer to prayer. It is a person's choice to celebrate the difference in others. HONOR IS THE SEED FOR ACCESS. It is trainable. Honor is the bridge to any season you want to enter into. **Success or Failure** can be traced to a person you honor or dishonor. Honor goes beyond personality. Even if you don't like the person – you should still honor them. Everyone has flaws – they are a part of our differences.

Weakness is the result of Principles ignored or ignorance of the Principles to apply. You never move past the period of instruction you disobey. Wisdom (Torah) – is the recognition of difference: right/wrong, good/evil, God/Satan. All wisdom is hidden so that the undeserving won't discover it. It is not acquired through academics; it is acquired through relationship. We prosper through honor; not wisdom. You cannot cast out, drive out or expel poverty. Honor must be introduced to get rid of poverty. Only honor can dispel POVERTY. Never pray for money, God will give you work. Pray for favor – money chases after you because you function by giving and receiving, sowing and reaping; not buying and selling.

Consequences of Dishonor

Dishonor – causes access to cut off immediately. God cast out Satan/Lucifer without another chance (Luk 10:19: Rev 12:7-9).

Dishonor – disqualifies; it is contagious and leads to poverty. Adam dishonored God and he was disqualified to stay in the garden. He was cast out of the garden to a life a hardship and suffering.

Dishonor – is destructive and destroys. It brings lack and poverty into the camp.

Dishonor – exposes Deception and the Deceiver. Pain (Hebrew root means – Deception) Deception is the birth place for all pain.

The first clue of **Dishonor** – is to request something unearned. E.g. Prodigal son Luke 15) – it led him into poverty. (Rabbi Ralph Messer) He should not have requested his inheritance; he should have waited until his father deemed him mature and ready. He requested what he could not handle. Fathers normally gave inheritances when they were close to death or about to die. He was implying that his father was taking too long to die or grow old.

Nine Steps to the Top (Rabbi Ralph Messer)

1. Crisis (Hebrew root means - Promotion) – produces opportunity
2. Opportunity – produce ministry
3. Ministry – produce favor
4. Favor- Promotion
5. Promotion – INCREASE
6. INCREASE – responsibility
7. Responsibility – Rewards
8. Rewards – attract attack
9. Attack – Crisis and back to number 1 above

The word enemy comes from the Hebrew root – meaning the one who announces the next level. The enemy determines your promotion. You are only rewarded for the enemy you overcome. God schedule enemies to keep you focus and provide an avenue for promotion – the less focus you are, the more enemies. When Satan wants to destroy your life he schedules a person for your life. When God wants you to succeed in life he schedules someone for you to HONOR in your life {**always watch who you are around – Abraham went to the next level after Lot**

(Veil) left}. Wisdom helps you to know the difference in an opportunity or a moment. ORDER dispels the enemy. Order is the accurate arrangement of all things. The closer you get to the source the more power and prosperity you have.

- Lucifer (Heb. Rt – son of honor). Pride comes in when someone receive honor that you desire for yourself. He wanted God's Honor for himself.
- Honor/Dishonor has a distinct scent.
- A principle applied accurately is called the **Law of Merit (excellence, quality, worthiness – it is the base for increase).** Principles always produce once they are followed correctly. God blesses those who walk by his principles. God is not a respecter of persons; but he is a respecter of principles. God has to abide by the principles he outlined in his words. Therefore, if we do as he directs, we will be qualified for his blessing or promises. This is not about working for salvation or blessings – it's about obedience.
- Freedom is the principles of God applied accurately (Jas 1:25). (Rabbi Ralph Messer)

PART 15: Managing Friendship and Relationships

Here are some principles you can reflect on and develop. Each one could be expanded to at least one page each; but I list them in point form.

1. Restoration rarely occurs after a decision of dishonor is made. It breaks trust.
2. Marriage failed because of **dishonor**; not adultery, and so forth.
3. When you **honor the right person** you will prosper.
4. **Delayed obedience** is the proof of Dishonor.
5. For everyone assigned to walk with you, one will walk against you.
6. **Two main** ways to learn: **Mentor or Mistake. Choose a mentor.**
7. The **slowest** way to learn: through **circumstances**
8. What you **refuse to learn from people**, you must learn **through pain**. It is a choice.
9. Let wrong relationships die.
10. **Wrong people never leave your life voluntarily** – you will have to make them leave or you leave.

11. God will **send or allow** wrong people in your life to teach you how to choose.

12. **A test** (Heb .– Nesaw… to make actual in your life)

13. **Identify** and **deal** with **disrespect**.

14. **Never** ignore the decision of a rebel.

15. **Never** entertain a rebel or else you are the rebel.

16. **Diligence** - the **workplace** and **proof** on honor.

17. Diligence – the immediate attention to an instruction.

18. **Diligence** gives you the power to obey an instruction.

19. ONLY the Diligent recognize and honor AUTHORITY and ONLY those in authority recognize and honor the diligent.

20. When people show you who they are **believe them**.

Using these principles to guide our life and choices will bring us into a better place with God and in life. People and wrong associations can set us back big time in life. Let us seek God's wisdom in every area of our life in the here and now. His name be praised.

Concluding Thoughts

Having read and applied the principles covered in this manual; make it your aim to be all God called you to be. You now realize that as a Son of God in the earth, you are precious to God. Your self esteem in God should be at a higher level knowing that you are a channel for God's grace, power and dominion in the earth. Your Spirit, Soul and Body should now be synchronized and better coordinated from God to your spirit. Keep training your spirit, keep the armour of God on, and use your gifts for God's glory and the edifying of the body of Christ. Balance your gifts with the fruit of the spirit. Let Christ be formed in you daily and live a life that honours God. Always work in harmony with the authority established by God. Always remember to whom much is given, much is required. You are now accountable for the new information you gained in this manual, don't let it remain with you. Go forth and help others fulfill their God-given purpose. God's richest blessings be yours.

Glossary

ἄνωθεν (anōthen)

Total KJV Occurrences: 14

Above, 6   Joh 3:31 (2), Joh 19:11, Jam 1:17, Jam 3:15, Jam 3:17

Again, 3 Joh 3:3, Joh 3:7, Gal 4:9

Top, 3 Mat 27:51, Mar 15:38, Joh 19:23

Beginning, 1 Act 26:5

First, 1 Luk 1:3

Γραφή (graphē)

Total KJV Occurrences: 51

scripture, 31 Mar 12:10, Mar 15:28, Joh 2:21-22 (2), Joh 7:38, Joh 7:42, Joh 10:35, Joh 13:18, Joh 17:12, Joh 19:24, Joh 19:28, Joh 19:36-37 (2), Joh 20:9, Act 1:16, Act 8:32, Act 8:35, Rom 4:3, Rom 9:17, Rom 10:11, Rom 11:2, Gal 3:8, Gal 3:22, Gal 4:30, 1Ti 5:18, 2Ti 3:16, Jam 2:8, Jam 2:23, Jam 4:5, 1Pe 2:6, 2Pe 1:20

scriptures, 20Mat 21:42, Mat 22:29, Mat 26:54, Mat 26:56, Mar 12:24, Mar 14:49, Luk 24:27, Luk 24:32, Luk 24:45, Joh5:39, Act 17:2, Act 17:11, Act 18:24, Act 18:28, Rom 1:2, Rom 15:4, Rom 16:26, 1Co 15:3-4 (2), 2Pe 3:16

γράφω (graphō)

Total KJV Occurrences: 194

written, 121 Mat 2:5, Mat 4:4, Mat 4:6-7 (2), Mat 11:10 (2), Mat 21:13, Mat 26:24, Mat 26:31, Mat 27:37, Mar 1:2, Mar 7:6, Mar 9:12-13 (2), Mar 11:17, Mar 14:21, Mar 14:27, Luk 2:23, Luk 4:4 (2), Luk 4:8, Luk 4:10, Luk 4:17, Luk 7:27, Luk 10:20, Luk 10:26, Luk 18:31, Luk 19:46, Luk 20:17, Luk 21:22, Luk 23:37-38 (2), Luk 24:44, Luk 24:46, Joh 2:17, Joh 6:31, Joh6:45, Joh 8:17, Joh 10:34, Joh 12:14, Joh 12:16, Joh 15:25, Joh 19:20, Joh 19:22 (2), Joh 20:30-31 (2), Joh 21:25 (2), Act 1:20, Act 7:42, Act 13:29, Act 13:33, Act 15:15, Act 23:5, Act 24:14, Rom 1:17, Rom 2:24, Rom 3:4, Rom 3:10, Rom 4:17, Rom 4:23, Rom 8:36, Rom 9:13, Rom 9:33, Rom 10:15, Rom 11:8, Rom 11:26, Rom 12:19, Rom 14:11, Rom 15:3, Rom 15:9, Rom 15:15, Rom 15:21, 1Co 1:19, 1Co 1:31, 1Co 2:9, 1Co3:19, 1Co 4:6, 1Co 5:11, 1Co 9:9-10 (2), 1Co 9:15, 1Co 10:7, 1Co 10:11, 1Co 14:21, 1Co 15:45, 1Co 15:54, 2Co 4:13, 2Co 8:15, 2Co 9:9, Gal 3:10 (2), Gal 3:13, Gal 4:22, Gal 4:27, Gal 6:11, Phm 1:19, Heb 10:7, 1Pe 1:16, 1Pe 5:12, 2Pe 3:15, 1Jo 2:14 (2), 1Jo 2:21, 1Jo 2:26, 1Jo 5:13, Rev 1:3, Rev 2:17, Rev 5:1, Rev 13:8, Rev 14:1, Rev 17:5, Rev 17:8, Rev 19:12, Rev 19:16, Rev 20:12, Rev 20:15, Rev 21:27, Rev 22:19

write, 50 Mar 10:4, Luk 1:3, Luk 16:6-7 (2), Joh 1:45, Joh 19:21, Act 25:26 (2), 1Co 4:14, 1Co 14:37, 2Co 1:13, 2Co 2:9, 2Co 13:1-2 (2), 2Co 13:10, Gal 1:20, Phi 3:1, 1Th 4:9, 1Th 5:1, 2Th 3:17, 1Ti 3:14, 2Pe 3:1, 1Jo 1:4,

116

1Jo 2:1, 1Jo 2:7-8 (2), 1Jo 2:12-13 (4), 2Jo 1:12, 3Jo 1:13 (2), Jud 1:3 (2), Rev 1:11, Rev 1:19, Rev 2:1, Rev 2:8, Rev 2:12, Rev 2:18, Rev 3:1, Rev 3:7, Rev 3:12, Rev 3:14, Rev 10:4 (2), Rev 14:13, Rev 19:9, Rev 21:5

wrote, 21　　Mar 10:5 (2), Mar 12:19, Luk 1:63, Luk 20:28, Joh 5:46, Joh 8:6, Joh 8:8, Joh 19:19, Joh 21:24, Act 15:23, Act 18:27, Act 23:25, Rom 16:22, 1Co 5:9, 1Co 7:1, 2Co 2:3-4 (2), 2Co 7:12, Phm 1:21, 2Jo 1:5, 3Jo 1:9

describeth, 1 Rom 10:5, **writing**, 1 Joh 19:19

ῥῆμα (rhēma)

Total KJV Occurrences: 73

words, 31　　Luk 20:26, Luk 24:8, Luk 24:11, Joh 3:34, Joh 5:47, Joh 6:63, Joh 6:68, Joh 8:20, Joh 8:47, Joh 10:21, Joh 12:47-48 (2), Joh 14:10, Joh 17:7-8 (2), Act 2:14, Act 5:20, Act 6:11, Act 6:13, Act 10:22, Act 10:44, Act 11:14, Act 13:42, Act 16:38, Act 26:25, Rom 10:18, 2Co 12:4, Heb 12:19, 2Pe 3:2, Rev 17:17 (2)

word, 28　　Mat 4:4, Mat 12:36, Mat 18:16, Mat 26:75, Mat 27:14, Mar 14:72, Luk 1:38, Luk 2:29, Luk 3:2, Luk 5:4-5 (2), Act 10:37, Act 11:16, Act 28:25, Rom 10:8 (2), Rom 10:17, 2Co 13:1, Gal 5:14, Gal 6:6, Eph 1:13, Eph 5:26, Eph 6:17, Heb 1:3, Heb 6:5, Heb 11:3, 1Pe 1:25 (2)

saying, 6　　Mar 9:32, Luk 2:17, Luk 2:50, Luk 9:45 (2), Luk 18:34

sayings, 3 Luk 1:65, Luk 2:51, Luk 7:1

things, 2 Luk 2:19, Act 5:32

evil, 1 Mat 5:11, nothing, 1 Luk 1:37

thing, 1 Luk 2:15,

Λόγος **(logos)**

Total KJV Occurrences: 325

word, 173   Mat 8:8, Mat 8:16, Mat 12:32, Mat 15:19-23 (7), Mat 22:46, Mar 2:2, Mar 4:14-16 (4), Mar 4:18-20 (3), Mar 4:33, Mar 5:36, Mar 7:13, Mar 16:20, Luk 1:2, Luk 4:32, Luk 4:36, Luk 5:1, Luk 7:7, Luk 8:11-13 (3), Luk 8:15, Luk 8:21, Luk 10:39, Luk 11:28, Luk 12:10, Luk 22:61, Luk 24:19, Joh 1:1 (3), Joh 1:14, Joh 2:22, Joh 4:41, Joh 4:50, Joh 5:24, Joh 5:38, Joh 8:31, Joh 8:37, Joh 8:43, Joh 10:35, Joh 12:48, Joh 14:24, Joh 15:3, Joh 15:20, Joh 15:25, Joh 17:6, Joh 17:14, Joh 17:17, Joh 17:20, Act 2:41, Act 4:4, Act 4:29, Act 4:31, Act 6:2, Act 6:4, Act 6:7, Act 8:4, Act 8:14, Act 8:25, Act 10:36, Act 10:44, Act 11:1, Act 11:19, Act 12:24, Act 13:5, Act 13:7, Act 13:15, Act 13:26, Act 13:44, Act 13:46, Act 13:48-49 (2), Act 14:3, Act 14:25, Act 15:7, Act 15:35-36 (2), Act 16:6, Act 16:32, Act 17:11, Act 17:13, Act 18:11, Act 19:10, Act 19:20, Act 20:32, Act 22:22, Rom 9:6, Rom 9:9, Rom 15:18, 1Co 4:20, 1Co 12:8 (2), 1Co 14:36, 2Co 1:18, 2Co 2:17, 2Co 4:2, 2Co 5:19, 2Co 6:7, 2Co 10:11, Phi 1:14, Phi 2:16, Col 1:5, Col 1:25, Col 3:16-17 (2), 1Th 1:5-6 (2), 1Th 1:8, 1Th 2:13 (3), 1Th 4:15, 2Th 2:2, 2Th 2:15,

2Th 2:17, 2Th 3:1, 2Th 3:14, 1Ti 4:5, 1Ti 4:12, 1Ti 5:17, 2Ti 2:9, 2Ti 2:15, 2Ti 2:17, 2Ti 4:2, Tit 1:3, Tit 1:9, Tit 2:5, Heb 4:2 (2), Heb 5:12-13 (2), Heb 7:28, Heb 12:19, Heb 13:7, Heb 13:22, Jam 1:18, Jam 1:21-23 (3), Jam 3:2, 1Pe 1:23, 1Pe 2:8, 1Pe 3:1 (2), 2Pe 1:19, 2Pe 3:5, 2Pe 3:7, 1Jo 1:1, 1Jo 1:10, 1Jo 2:5, 1Jo 2:7, 1Jo 2:14, 1Jo 3:18, 1Jo 5:7, Rev 1:2, Rev 1:9, Rev 3:8, Rev 3:10, Rev 6:9, Rev 12:11, Rev 19:13, Rev 20:4

words, 48   Mat 10:14, Mat 12:37 (2), Mat 24:35, Mat 26:44, Mar 8:38, Mar 10:24, Mar 12:13, Mar 13:31, Mar 14:39, Luk 1:20, Luk 3:4, Luk 4:22, Luk 9:26, Luk 20:20, Luk 21:33, Luk 23:9, Luk 24:44, Joh 14:23, Act 2:22, Act 2:40, Act 5:5, Act 7:22, Act 15:15, Act 15:24, Act 15:32, Act 18:15, Act 20:35, Act 20:38, 1Co 1:17, 1Co 2:4, 1Co 2:13, 1Co 14:9, 1Co 14:19 (2), Eph 5:6, 1Th 2:5, 1Th 4:18, 1Ti 4:6, 1Ti 6:3, 2Ti 1:13, 2Ti 4:15, 2Pe 2:3, 3Jo 1:10, Rev 1:3, Rev 21:5, Rev 22:18-19 (2)

saying, 33 Mat 15:12, Mat 19:11, Mat 19:22, Mat 28:15, Mar 7:29, Mar 8:32, Mar 9:10, Mar 10:22, Luk 1:29, Joh 4:37, Joh 4:39, Joh 6:60, Joh 7:36, Joh 7:40, Joh 8:51, Joh 8:55, Joh 12:38, Joh 15:20, Joh 18:9, Joh 18:32, Joh 19:8, Joh 19:13, Joh 21:23, Act 6:5, Act 7:29, Act 16:36, Rom 13:9, 1Co 15:54, 1Ti 1:15, 1Ti 3:1, 1Ti 4:9, 2Ti 2:11, Tit 3:8

sayings, 16 Mat 7:24, Mat 7:26, Mat 7:28, Mat 26:1 (2), Luk 6:47, Luk 9:28, Luk 9:44, Joh 10:19, Joh 14:24, Rom 3:4, Rev 19:9, Rev 22:6-7 (2), Rev 22:9-10 (2)

account, 8 Mat 12:36, Mat 18:23, Luk 16:2, Act 19:40, Rom 14:12, Heb 13:17 (2), 1Pe 4:5

speech, 8 Act 20:7, 1Co 2:1, 1Co 2:4, 1Co 4:19, 2Co 10:10, 2Co 11:6, Col 4:6, Tit 2:8

matter, 4 Mar 1:45, Act 8:21, Act 15:6, Act 19:38

utterance, 4 1Co 1:5, 2Co 8:7, Eph 6:19, Col 4:3

things, 3 Luk 1:3-4 (2), Act 20:24 (2)

communication, 2 Mat 5:37, Eph 4:29

reason, 2 Act 18:14, 1Pe 3:15, **thing**, 2 Mat 21:24, Luk 20:3

work, 2 Rom 9:28 (2), **cause**, 1 Mat 5:32, **communications**, 1 Luk 24:17

concerning, 1 Phi 4:15, do, 1 Heb 4:13

doctrine, 1 Heb 6:1, **fame**, 1 Luk 5:15, **intent**, 1 Act 10:29

mouth, 1 Act 15:27, **move**, 1 Act 20:24, **preaching**, 1 1Co 1:18

question, 1 Mar 11:29, **reckoneth**, 1 Mat 25:19

rumour, 1 Luk 7:17, **say**, 1 Heb 5:11

show, 1 Col 2:23, **speaker**, 1 Act 14:12,

talk, 1 Mat 22:15, **tidings**, 1 Act 11:22

treatise, 1 Act 1:1, **word's**, 1 Mar 4:17

Reference List

Capps. C. (1995). *The Tongue – A Creative Force.* Oklahoma: Harrison House Inc.

Flow Chart of The Spiritual Maturation Process. Retrieved from April 9, 2015 http://www.brainout.net/SMP.doc

Hagin, K. E. (1978). How You Can Be Led By The Spirit of God. USA: Kenneth Hagin Ministries

_____ . (1985). *The Human Spirit: Volume 2 of the Spirit, Soul, and Body Series.* USA: Faith Library Publications

Messer, Ralf. *Sermon*

_____ . www.torah.tv

Nee, Watchman. (1972). *Spiritual Authority.* New York: Christian Fellowship Publishers, Inc.

_____ . (1968). *The Spiritual Man: In three Volumes.* New York: Christian Publishers, INC.

Oyedepo, Dr. David. *Sermon*

Pryce, Frederick K. C. (sr). *The Armour of God.* Ever Increasing Faith Broadcast – TBN

Notes

Notes